THE BEST AND BIGGEST FUN WORK BOOK FOR MINECRAFTERS

Grades 3 & 4

Illustrated by Amanda Brack

Sky Pony Press
New York

Sky Pony Press books may be purchased in bulk at special discounts for sales promotion, corporate gifts, fund-raising, or educational purposes. Special editions can also be created to specifications. For details, contact the Special Sales Department, Sky Pony Press, 307 West 36th Street, 11th Floor, New York, NY 10018 or info@skyhorsepublishing.com.

Sky Pony® is a registered trademark of Skyhorse Publishing, Inc.®, a Delaware corporation.

Minecraft® is a registered trademark of Notch Development AB.
The Minecraft game is copyright © Mojang AB.

Visit our website at www.skyponypress.com.

10 9 8 7 6 5 4 3 2

Library of Congress Cataloging-in-Publication Data is available on file.

Cover design by Brian Peterson

Interior and cover art by Amanda Brack

Book design by Kevin Baier

Print ISBN: 978-1-5107-4497-4

Printed in the United States of America

A NOTE TO PARENTS

Welcome to a great big world of fun and learning with a Minecrafting twist. When you want to reinforce classroom skills, break up screen time, or enhance kids' problem-solving skills at home, it's crucial to have high-interest, kid-friendly learning materials.

The Best and Biggest Fun Workbook for Minecrafters transforms educational lessons into exciting adventures complete with diamond swords, zombies, skeletons, and creepers. With colorful illustrations and familiar characters to guide them through, your kids will feel like winners from start to finish.

This mega-fun workbook is organized into five distinct chapters targeting a wide variety of math, reading, spelling, writing, science, S.T.E.M. skills, and more. Inside you'll find exercises in math basics like skip counting; spelling activities that improve reading fluency, guided narrative, expository, and opinion writing instruction, S.T.E.M. challenges to encourage curiosity and problem-solving skills, and a full review that covers key concepts in reading, writing, math, and science. Use the table of contents to pinpoint areas for extra practice!

Now for the best part: The educational content in this workbook is aligned with National Common Core Standards for 3rd and 4th grade. What does that mean, exactly? Everything in this book matches up with what your children are learning or will be learning in third and fourth grade. This eliminates confusion, builds confidence, and keeps them ahead of the curve.

Whether it's the joy of seeing their favorite game come to life on each page or the thrill of solving challenging problems just like Steve and Alex, there is something in *The Best and Biggest Fun Workbook for Minecrafters* to entice every student.

Happy adventuring!

CONTENTS

CHAPTER ONE

MATH FOR MINECRAFTERS

MULTIPLICATION BY GROUPING

Write the multiplication sentence that matches the picture. Then solve the equation.

Example:

1.

Answer:

$$\underline{3} \times \underline{5} = \underline{15}$$

2. $\underline{8} \times \underline{2} = \underline{16}$

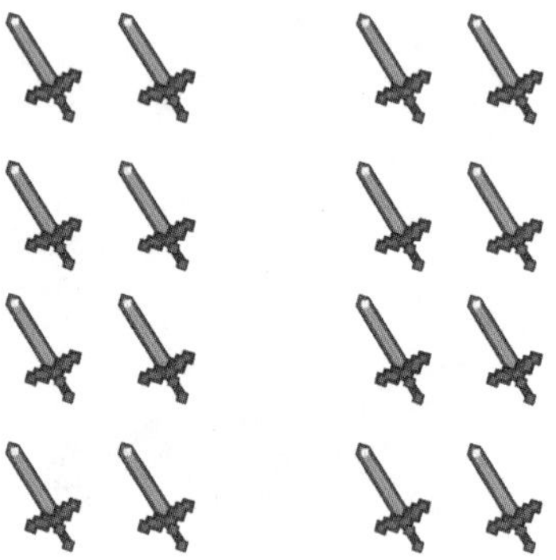

3. $\underline{6} \times \underline{4} = \underline{24}$

4. $\underline{3} \times \underline{4} = \underline{12}$

5. $\underline{7} \times \underline{5} = \underline{35}$

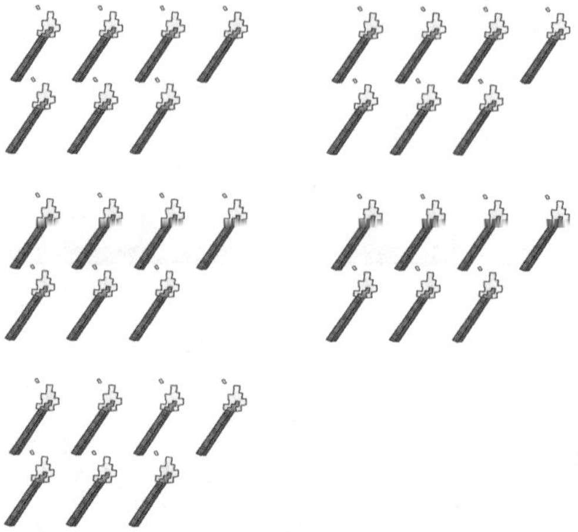

MATH FACTS CHALLENGE

Find the pattern and fill in the empty spaces to help Steve escape the creeper.

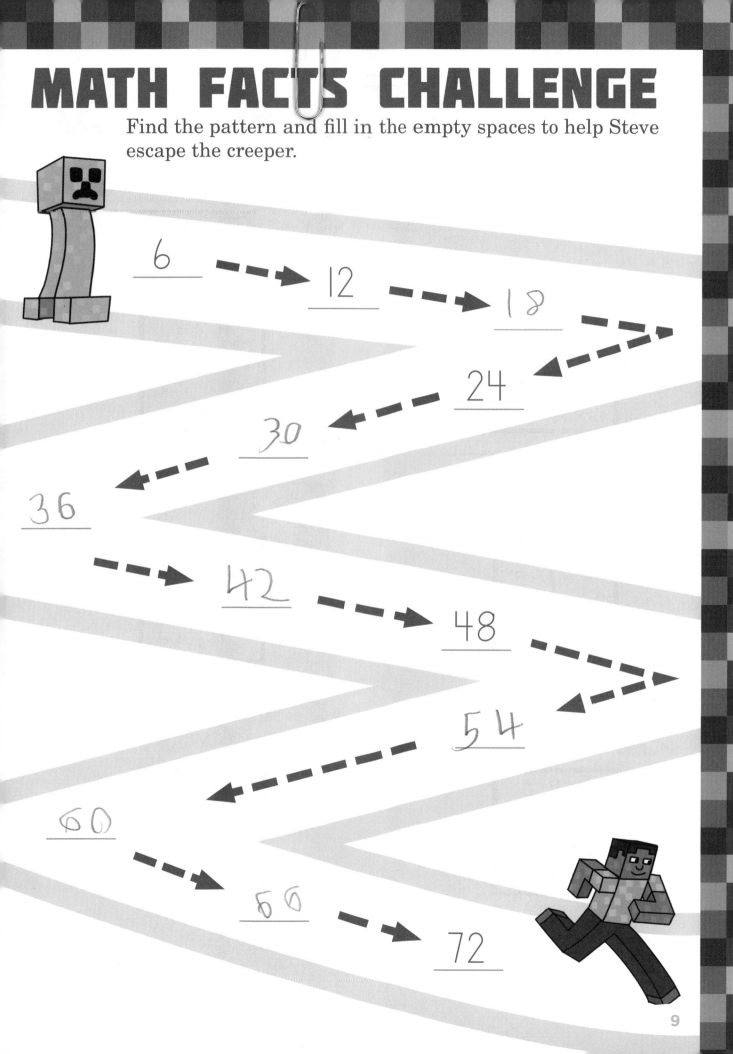

6 → 12 → 18

24

30

36

42 → 48

54

60

66 → 72

TELLING TIME

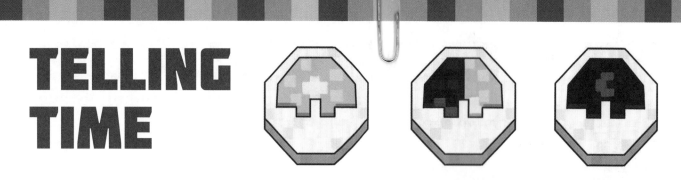

Look at the clocks below and write the time in the space provided:

Example:

1.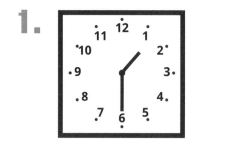

Answer: 1:30

2.

Answer: 3:15

3.

Answer: 12:25

4.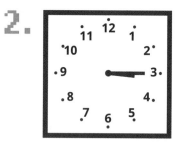

Answer: 6:40

5.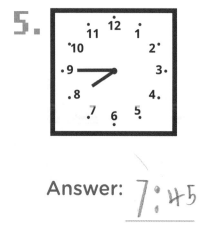

Answer: 7:45

6.

Answer: 2:05

THE TRADING TABLE

The villagers have emeralds to give Alex in exchange for her food items. Look at the table below to solve the problems that follow.

FISHERMAN	🟢	🟢				
SHEPHERD	🟢	🟢	🟢	🟢	🟢	
TOOL SMITH	🟢	🟢	🟢	🟢		
CLERIC	🟢	🟢	🟢	🟢	🟢	🟢

Write the amount of emeralds next to each villager using the table above.

1 pile of emeralds = 7 emeralds.

1. The **fisherman** villager has ___14___ .

2. The **shepherd** villager has ___35___ .

3. The **tool smith** villager has ___28___ .

4. The **cleric** villager has ___42___ .

5. Which villagers have more emeralds than the **tool smith** villager? ___Shepherd, Cleric___

6. Which villager has the least amount of emeralds? ___Fisherman___

7. The **fisherman** wants to have as many emeralds as the **cleric**. Which villager's collection does she need to add to hers? ___Tool Smith___

11

GEOMETRY SKILLS PRACTICE

How many items are in each array? Count the number of items in one row and one column. Write a multiplication sentence to find the answer.

Example:

1. 2 × 4 = 8

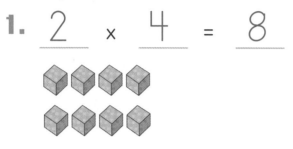

2. 3 × 5 = 15

3. 3 × 9 = 27

4. 5 × 7 = 35

5. 2 × 6 = 12

6. __4__ x __5__ = __20__

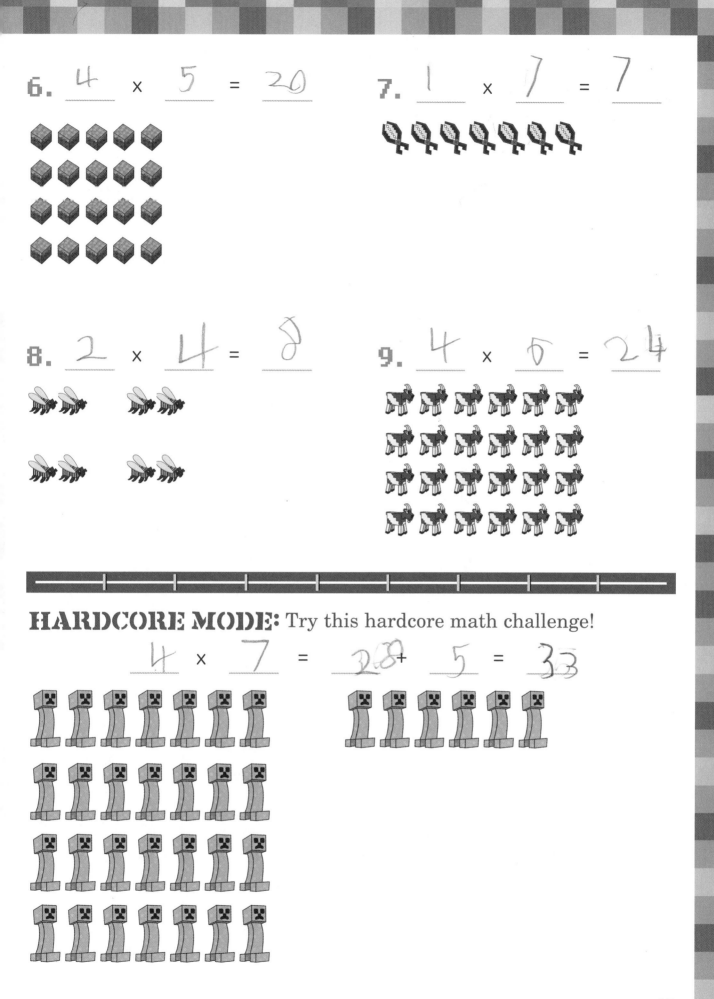

7. __1__ x __7__ = __7__

8. __2__ x __4__ = __8__

9. __4__ x __6__ = __24__

HARDCORE MODE: Try this hardcore math challenge!

__4__ x __7__ = __28__ + __5__ = __33__

MULTIPLICATION WORD PROBLEMS

Read the problem carefully. Draw a picture or write a number sentence to help you solve the problem.

Example:

1. A zombie villager needs to be fed 2 golden apples to turn back into a villager. How many apples do you need to cure 3 zombie villagers?

Answer: 6 golden apples

3 x 2 = 6

2. You need 8 diamonds to make 1 chestplate. How many diamonds do you need to make 2 chestplates?

Answer: 16

3. You need 4 grass blocks to make a path along 1 side of your square house. How many grass blocks do you need to make a path on 4 sides of your house?

Answer: 16

4. A cow gives 3 buckets of milk per day. How many buckets of milk will you have after 7 days?

Answer: 21

5. A chicken lays 4 eggs a day. How many eggs will you have at the end of the day if your farm has 5 chickens?

Answer: 20

6. You need 9 wood blocks to make 1 large crafting table. How many wood blocks do you need to make 3 large crafting tables?

Answer: 27

7. A total of 3 TNT blocks will destroy 1 creeper. How many TNT blocks do you need to destroy 5 creepers?

Answer: 15

8. Alex uses 1 carrot to tame 1 pig. How many carrots will she need to tame 7 pigs?

Answer: 7

9. You need 3 blocks of snow to make 1 snow golem. How many blocks of snow do you need to make 6 snow golems?

Answer: 18

SNOW GOLEM'S GUIDE TO PLACE VALUE

Answer the multiplication questions below.
Then round to the closest ten.

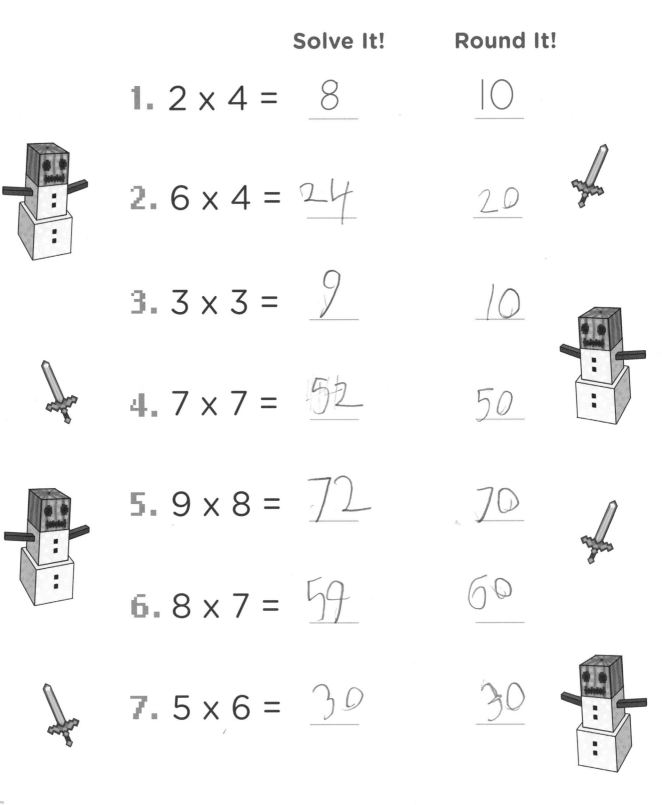

	Solve It!	**Round It!**
1. 2 x 4 =	8	10
2. 6 x 4 =	24	20
3. 3 x 3 =	9	10
4. 7 x 7 =	52	50
5. 9 x 8 =	72	70
6. 8 x 7 =	59	60
7. 5 x 6 =	30	30

MATH FACTS CHALLENGE

Count by 3 and practice your math facts to help the ocelot get the fish.

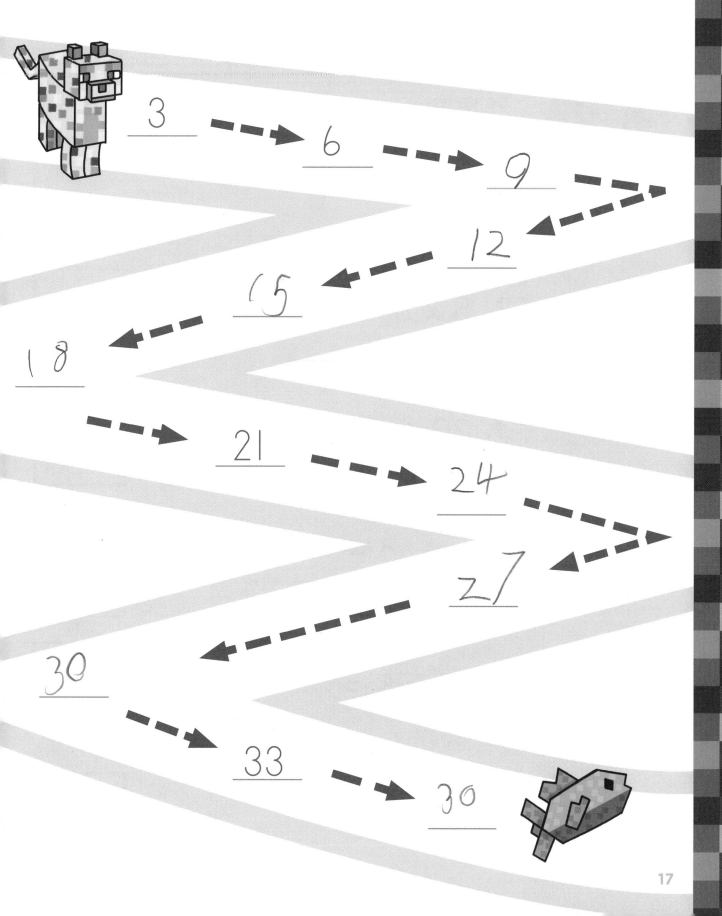

3

6

9

12

15

18

21

24

27

30

33

30

MINUTE HAND MYSTERY

A computer glitch erased the minute hands from these clocks! Solve the problem to find out how many minutes have passed, then draw in the minute hand.

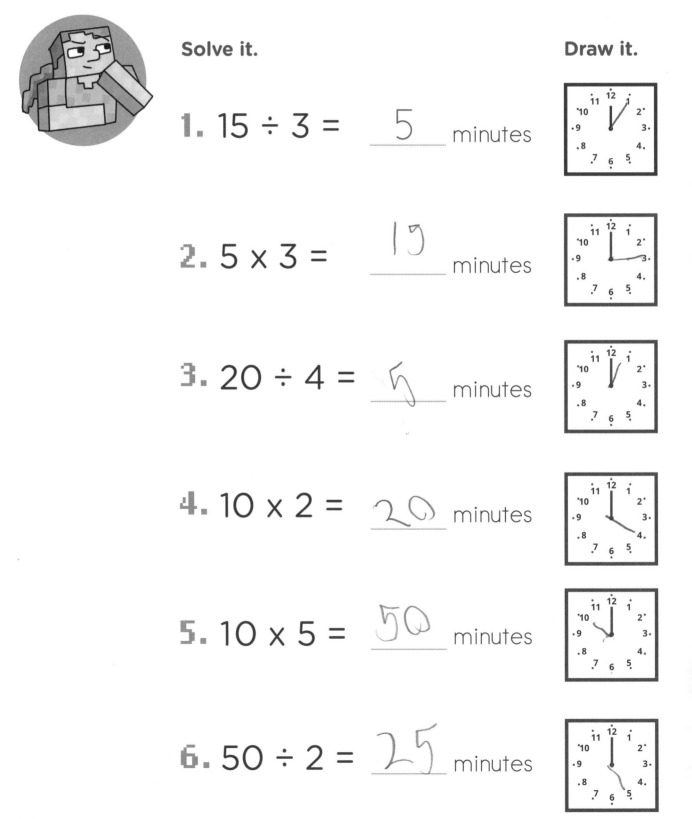

Solve it.

Draw it.

1. $15 \div 3 =$ ___5___ minutes

2. $5 \times 3 =$ ___15___ minutes

3. $20 \div 4 =$ ___5___ minutes

4. $10 \times 2 =$ ___20___ minutes

5. $10 \times 5 =$ ___50___ minutes

6. $50 \div 2 =$ ___25___ minutes

EQUAL TRADE

This librarian villager loves trading for new coins. Figure out the right number of coins to trade so that you don't lose any money in the deal.

1. How many **nickels** equal 1 dime?      Answer: 2

2. How many **pennies** equal 1 quarter?   Answer: 25

3. How many **nickels** equal 2 dimes?      Answer: 4

4. How many **dimes** equal a dollar?   Answer: 10

5. How many **pennies** equal 2 quarters?   Answer: 50

ADVENTURES IN GEOMETRY

Which of these gaming images are symmetrical?
Circle the number.

Symmetrical = an object that can be divided with a line into two matching halves.

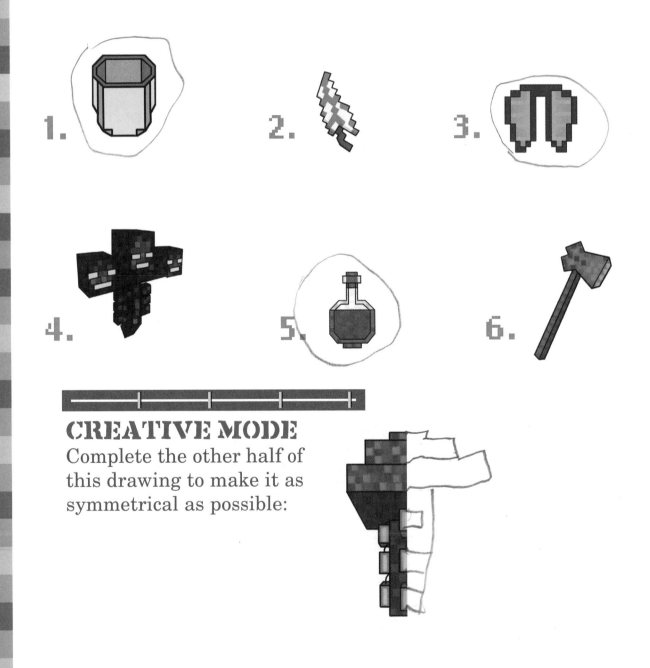

1.

2.

3.

4.

5.

6.

CREATIVE MODE

Complete the other half of
this drawing to make it as
symmetrical as possible:

SHELTER GEOMETRY

Alex and Steve have been working all afternoon to build a new shelter out of redstone blocks.

Area = height x width

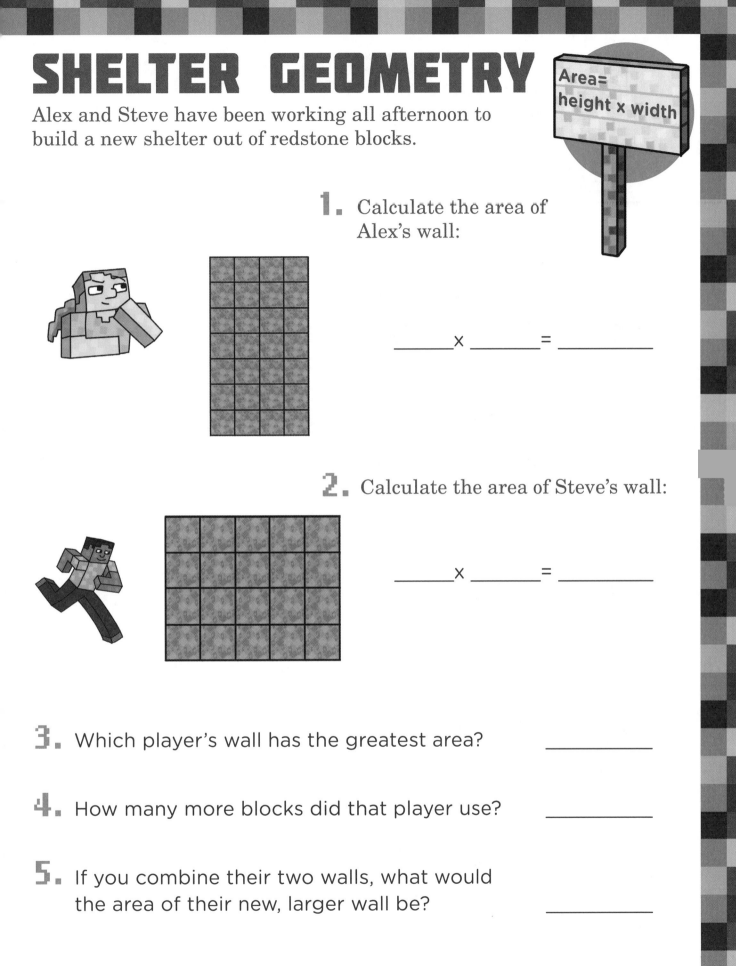

1. Calculate the area of Alex's wall:

_____ x _____ = _____

2. Calculate the area of Steve's wall:

_____ x _____ = _____

3. Which player's wall has the greatest area? _____

4. How many more blocks did that player use? _____

5. If you combine their two walls, what would the area of their new, larger wall be? _____

MULTIPLICATION BY GROUPING

Count each group of 4, then finish the equation to find the answer.

1.

$$\underline{3} \times 4 = \underline{12}$$

2.

$$\underline{5} \times 4 = \underline{20}$$

3.

$$\underline{4} \times 4 = \underline{16}$$

4.

$$\underline{2} \times 4 = \underline{8}$$

5.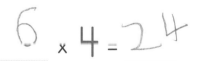

$$\underline{6} \times 4 = \underline{24}$$

MYSTERY MESSAGE
WITH MULTIPLICATION AND DIVISION

Solve the problems below to find out which number matches with which letter. Then put the correct letters into the message to answer the riddle!

1. $136 \div 2 =$ <u>68</u> E

2. $27 \times 4 =$ _____ O

3. $32 \times 3 =$ _____ H

4. $623 \div 7 =$ _____ R

5. $124 \times 6 =$ _____ B

6. $256 \div 8 =$ _____ N

7. $103 \times 9 =$ _____ I

8. $248 \div 8 =$ _____ G

9. $62 \times 6 =$ _____ S

Q: What do you call horses that linger near your structure?
COPY THE LETTERS FROM THE ANSWERS ABOVE TO FIND OUT.

<u>32</u>   <u>68</u>   <u>927</u>   <u>31</u>   <u>96</u>   <u>744</u>   <u>108</u>   <u>89</u>   <u>372</u>

GHAST'S GUIDE TO PLACE VALUE

Solve the multiplication equations below. Match each answer to the correct place value description on the right.

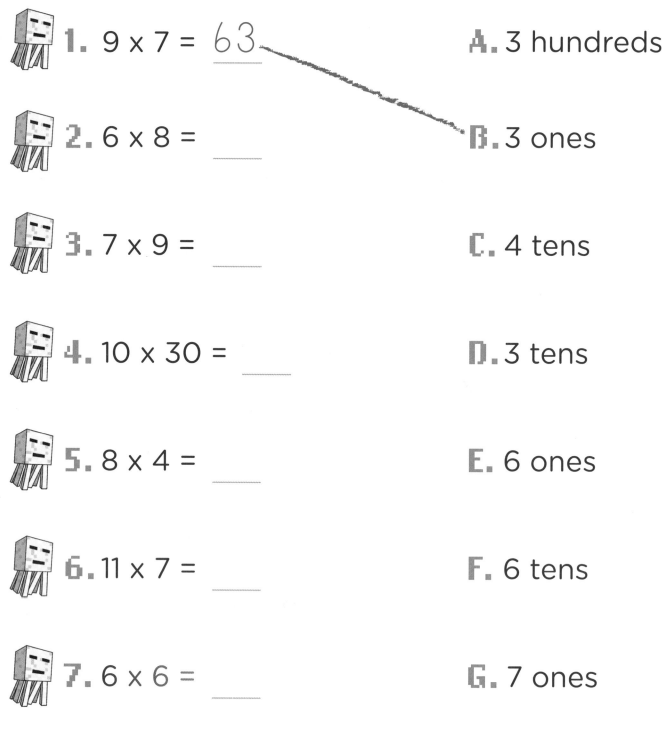

1. $9 \times 7 = $ 63

2. $6 \times 8 = $ ___

3. $7 \times 9 = $ ___

4. $10 \times 30 = $ ___

5. $8 \times 4 = $ ___

6. $11 \times 7 = $ ___

7. $6 \times 6 = $ ___

A. 3 hundreds

B. 3 ones

C. 4 tens

D. 3 tens

E. 6 ones

F. 6 tens

G. 7 ones

SKIP COUNT CHALLENGE

You have the right light levels to grow 5 mushrooms each day. Count by 5 to find out how many mushrooms you'll have at the end of 12 days.

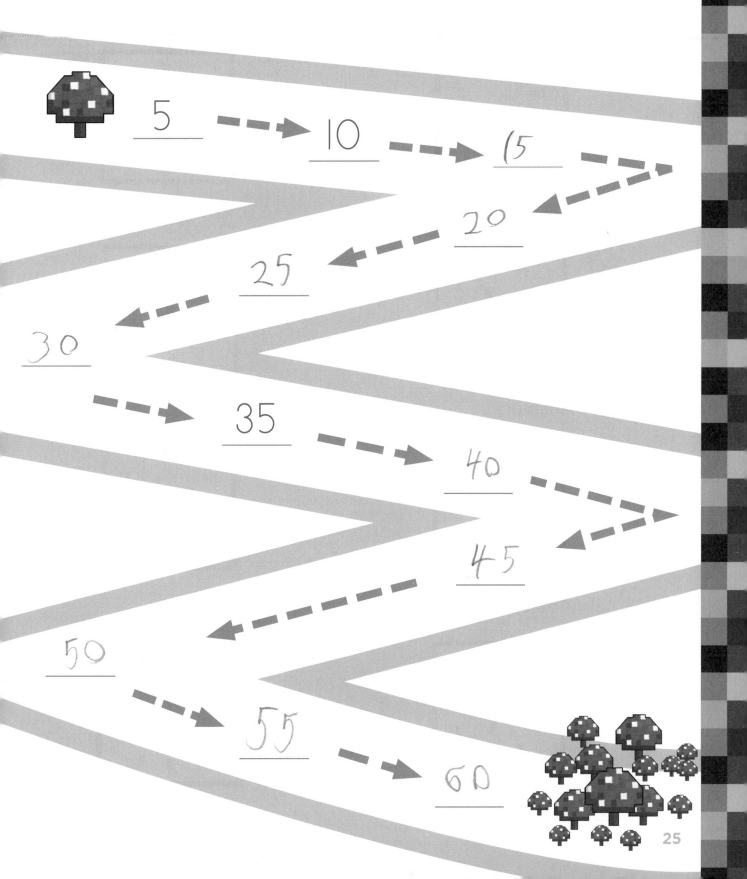

5 → 10 → 15 → 20 → 25 → 30 → 35 → 40 → 45 → 50 → 55 → 60

TELLING TIME

The baby zombie is learning how to tell time but needs your help. Help the baby zombie by writing down the correct time next to each clock.

Example:

1.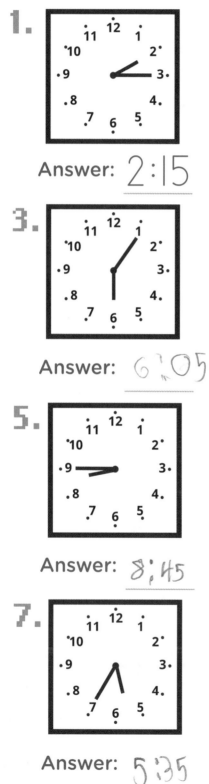

Answer: 2:15

2.

Answer: 3:30

3.

Answer: 6:05

4.

Answer: 11:20

5.

Answer: 8:45

6.

Answer: 10:10

7.

Answer: 5:35

8.

Answer: 12:00

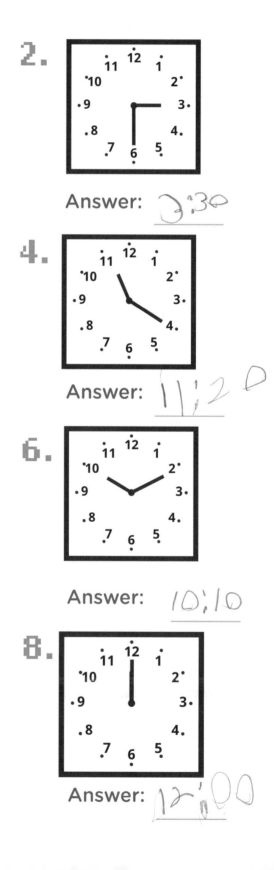

SPAWN EGG CHALLENGE

Solve the equations next to each colored bucket to find out how many exploding creepers will soon be hatching from the buckets. Then run!

1. $23 \times 5 =$ _____

2. $180 \div 3 =$ _____

3. $94 \times 3 =$ _____

4. $45 \times 4 =$ _____

5. $216 \div 9 =$ _____

6. $13 \times 6 =$ _____

7. Which colored bucket has the most creeper eggs? _____

8. Which two colored buckets, when combined, add up to 102 creeper eggs? _____ and _____

HARDCORE MODE: Try this hardcore math challenge!

9. What is the sum of all the creeper eggs? _____

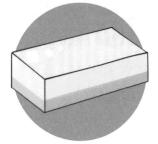

EQUAL PARTS CHALLENGE

Use a ruler or the edge of a piece of paper to help you draw partitions in the shapes below.

When you partition something, you divide it into sections

1. The first gold ingot below is partitioned, or divided, into **3** equal parts with the red line.

2. There is another way to divide this gold ingot into **3** equal, symmetrical parts.
Draw it below:

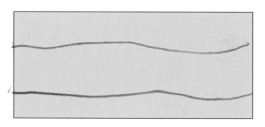

3. Use your pencil to shade in one of the pieces above. What fraction describes this picture? 1/3

4. Partition the iron ingot into **4** equal shares in two different ways.

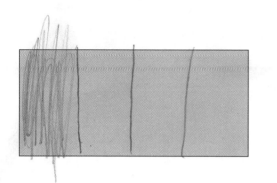

Use your pencil to shade in one of the pieces above. What fraction describes this picture?   1 / 4

5. Partition the iron ingot into **6** equal shares in two different ways.

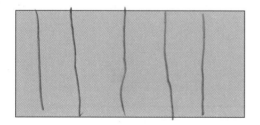
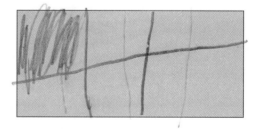

Use your pencil to shade in one of the pieces above. What fraction describes this picture? $\frac{1}{6}$

MYSTERY MESSAGE WITH MULTIPLICATION

Solve each multiplication equation below. Use the answers to solve the riddle.

1. 26
   ×9
   234

   U

2. 38
   ×7

   J

3. 54
   ×8

   Y

4. 27
   ×6

   B

5. 42
   ×5

   F

6. 49
   ×8

   I

7. 19
   ×7

   E

8. 95
   ×5

   C

Q: Where does Steve go to get his cart serviced?
COPY THE LETTERS FROM THE ANSWERS ABOVE TO FIND OUT.

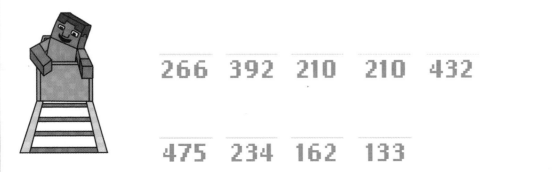

266 392 210 210 432

475 234 162 133

MULTIPLICATION AND DIVISION MYSTERY NUMBER

Some hacker has replaced a number from each of the below equations with a pufferfish. Use multiplication and division to solve for the missing numbers.

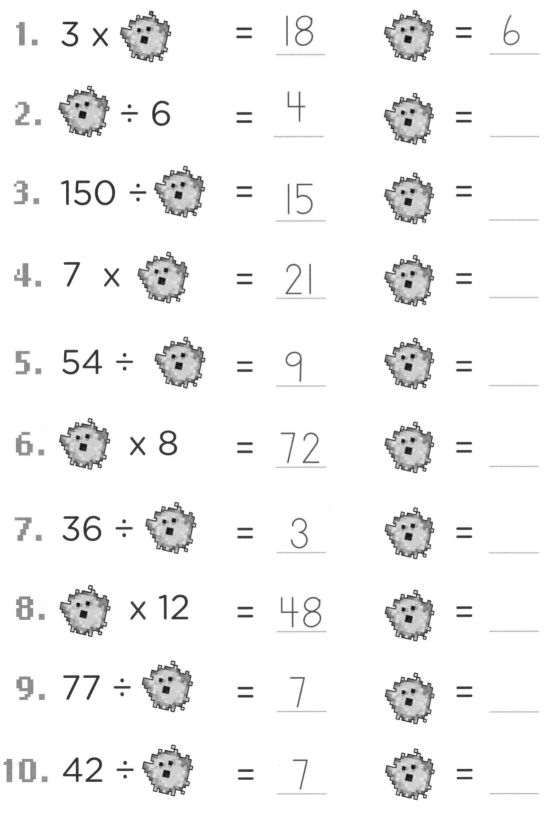

1. 3 x  = 18  = 6
2.  ÷ 6 = 4  = ____
3. 150 ÷  = 15  = ____
4. 7 x  = 21  = ____
5. 54 ÷  = 9  = ____
6.  x 8 = 72  = ____
7. 36 ÷  = 3  = ____
8.  x 12 = 48  = ____
9. 77 ÷  = 7  = ____
10. 42 ÷  = 7  = ____

ENDER DRAGON'S NUMBER CHALLENGE

Match the Ender Dragon with the description of the number.

1. Hundreds: **1** Tens: **6** Ones: **2**

A.  633÷3

2. Hundreds: **2** Tens: **1** Ones: **1**

B. 42x8

3. Hundreds: **4** Tens: **4** Ones: **8**

C.  18x9

4. Hundreds: **3** Tens: **3** Ones: **6**

D.  795÷5

5. Hundreds: **1** Tens: **5** Ones: **9**

E.  64x7

SKIP COUNT CHALLENGE

Three zombie villagers are after you. Count by 4 to find the splash potion of weakness and cure them.

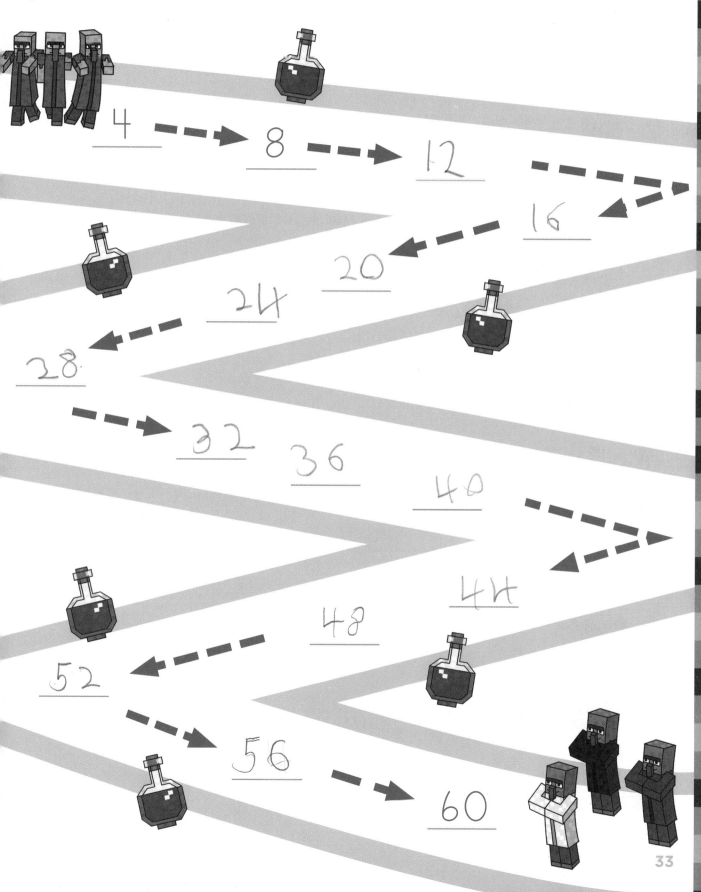

4 → 8 → 12 → 16 → 20 → 24 → 28 → 32 → 36 → 40 → 44 → 48 → 52 → 56 → 60

CREATING POTIONS

Use the recipes below to figure out the number of items needed to make more of each potion.

1.  = 4 awkward potions + 2 glistering melons

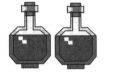 = _____ awkward potions +

_____ glistering melons

2. = 3 awkward potions + 6 sugars

 = _____ awkward potions + _____ sugars

3. = 5 golden carrots + 8 nether warts

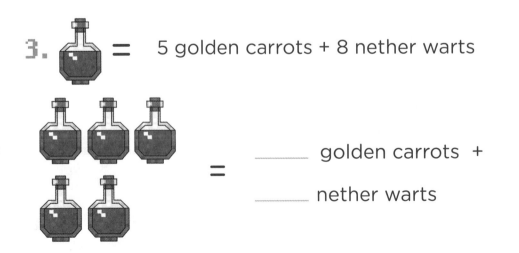 = _____ golden carrots +

_____ nether warts

34

INVISIBILITY POTION FORMULA

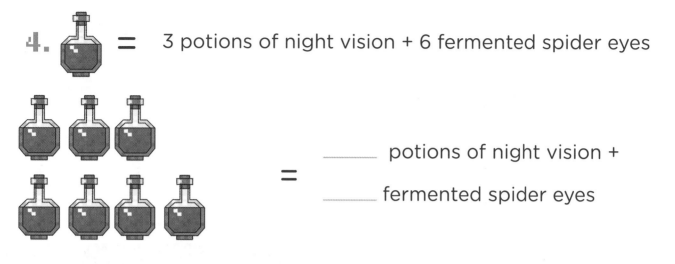

4. 🧪 = 3 potions of night vision + 6 fermented spider eyes

🧪🧪🧪
🧪🧪🧪🧪
= _____ potions of night vision +

_____ fermented spider eyes

INVISIBILITY POTION INGREDIENTS TABLE

Use the formula above to determine how much you need of each ingredient below. The first one is done for you.

Night Vision Potion	6			
Fermented Spider Eyes				

ADVENTURES IN GEOMETRY: PERIMETER AND AREA

Alex is building new rooms in her house. Multiply the number of blocks to help her find the perimeter and area of the walls.

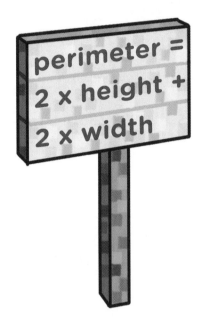

perimeter =
2 x height +
2 x width

1. Perimeter = _____

If Alex triples the height of this wall,

what would the new perimeter be? _____

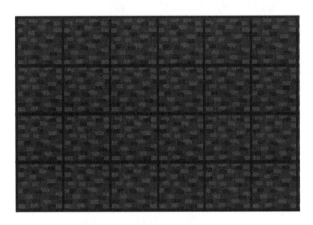

2. Perimeter = _____

If Alex destroys the right half of this wall,

what would the new perimeter be? _____

3. Perimeter = _____

Alex built a wall twice as wide as this one.

What was the perimeter of her new wall?

_____

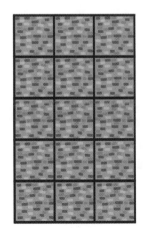

area = height × width

4. Area = _____

If Alex doubles the height of this wall, what would the new area be? _____

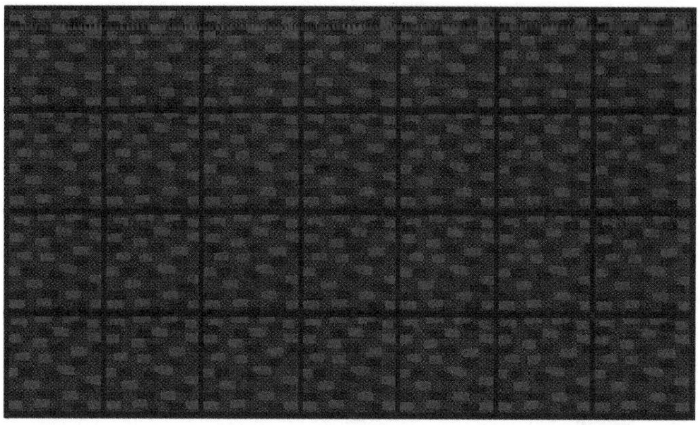

5. Area = _____

If Alex destroys the right half of this wall, what would the new area be? _____

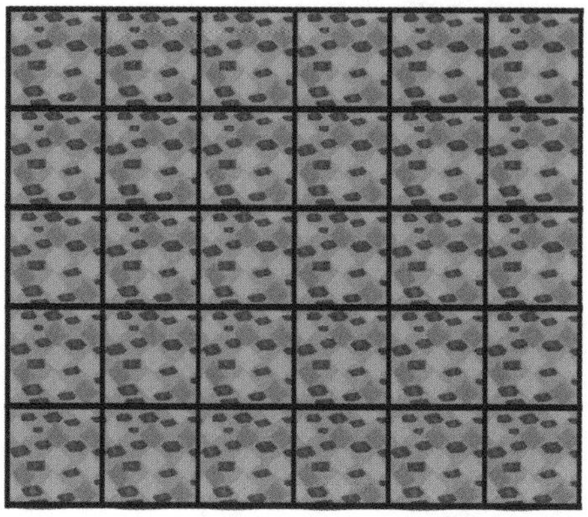

6. Area = _____

Alex built a wall twice as tall as this one. What was the area of her wall? _____

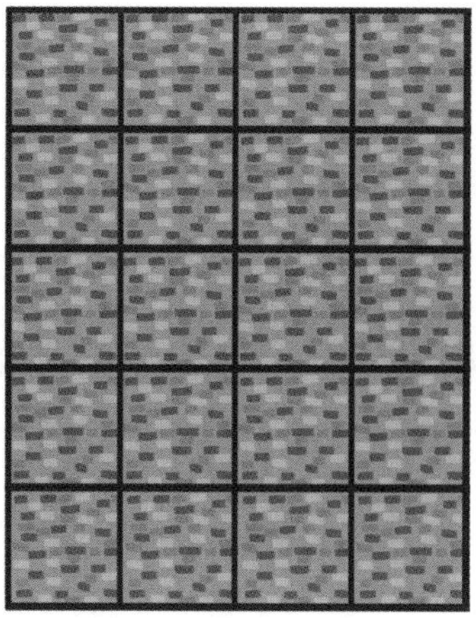

WORD PROBLEMS

Use multiplication and division to solve these word problems.

1. Alex must feed her pig 4 carrots before she can ride it. If she wants to ride her pig 7 times, how many carrots does she need?

Answer: _28_

2. Steve needs 3 diamonds to craft a diamond sword. How many diamonds will he need to craft 9 diamond swords?

Answer: _27_

3. As you explore the Plains biome, you pass 2 different groups of 12 flowers. How many flowers do you pass in all?

Answer: _24_

4. Steve is mining for iron ore. He breaks each block into 6 pieces. In the end he has 30 pieces of ore. How many blocks did he start with?

Answer: _5_

5. Each melon block drops 4 slices and each slice is cut into 3 pieces. If you have 5 melon blocks, how many melon pieces will you get?

Answer: 6_0

6. If Alex's bow shoots 6 enchanted arrows per hour and Steve's bow shoots 4, how many arrows total will they shoot in 8 hours?

Answer: 80

7. Alex has 3 bees. Each bee breeds 4 baby bees in one hour. How many bees does Alex have at the end of 3 hours?

Answer: 45

8. Steve and Alex lose 3 damage hearts each time they battle a spider. One day, they both fight 3 spiders. How many hearts do they lose in all?

Answer: 18

PLACE VALUE

Match the answer to each equation on the left with the number of flowers on the right to help Steve calculate how many flowers he planted in total.

1. 7 x 3 x 8 = _____

2. 13 x 8 x 6 = _____

3. 14 x 7 x 3 = _____

4. 5 x 10 x 7 = _____

5. 12 x 7 x 5 = _____

6. 9 x 11 x 5 = _____

7. 26 x 4 x 8 = _____

A. 350

B. 168

C. 624

D. 495

E. 832

F. 420

G. 294

SQUID NUMBER CHALLENGE

Match the answer to the equation on the right with the correct place value description on the left.

1. Hundreds: **1** Tens: **8** Ones: **0**

2. Hundreds: **1** Tens: **0** Ones: **3**

3. Hundreds: **2** Tens: **2** Ones: **8**

4. Hundreds: **7** Tens: **3** Ones: **8**

5. Hundreds: **3** Tens: **3** Ones: **6**

6. Hundreds: **2** Tens: **9** Ones: **4**

7. Hundreds: **0** Tens: **9** Ones: **1**

A. 76 x 3

B. 82 x 9

C. 14 x 21

D. 309 ÷ 3

E. 546 ÷ 6

F. 36 x 5

G. 42 x 8

MOB MEASUREMENTS

Use multiplication and addition to measure the height of each animal.

1 foot = 12 inches

Example:

1.

Goat
2 feet, 6 inches

12 x 2 = 24 inches

24 + 6 = 30 inches tall

2.

Pig
2 feet, 2 inches

Height in inches = 6

3.

Cow
3 feet, 5 inches

Height in inches = 20

4.

Sheep

3 feet, 8 inches

Height in inches = _____

5.

Chicken

1 foot, 9 inches

Height in inches = _____

METRIC MEASUREMENTS

Complete the chart using the formula provided.

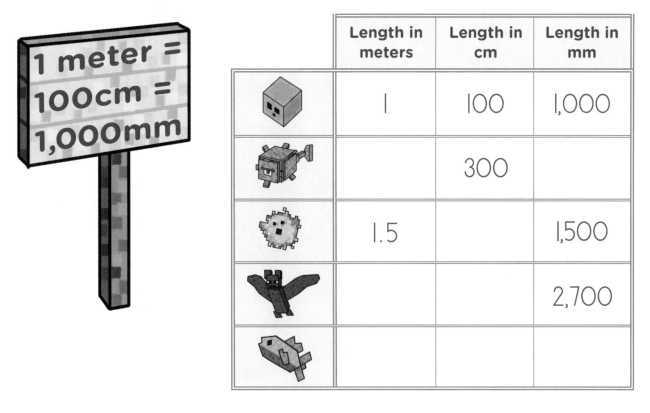

1 meter =
100cm =
1,000mm

	Length in meters	Length in cm	Length in mm
	1	100	1,000
		300	
	1.5		1,500
			2,700

ADVENTURES IN GEOMETRY

Identify the angle shown in each picture as acute, right, or obtuse.

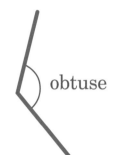 obtuse

 acute

 right

1. obtuse

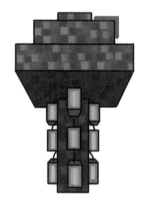

2. right

3. right

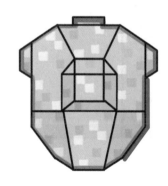

4. obtuse

5. <u>acute</u>

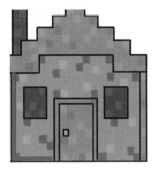

6. right

7. <u>obtuse</u>

8. obtuse

MULTIPLICATION AND DIVISION MYSTERY NUMBER

A troublesome creeper has replaced a number in each equation with a creeper spawn egg! Use multiplication and division to determine the missing number.

1. $248 \div$ 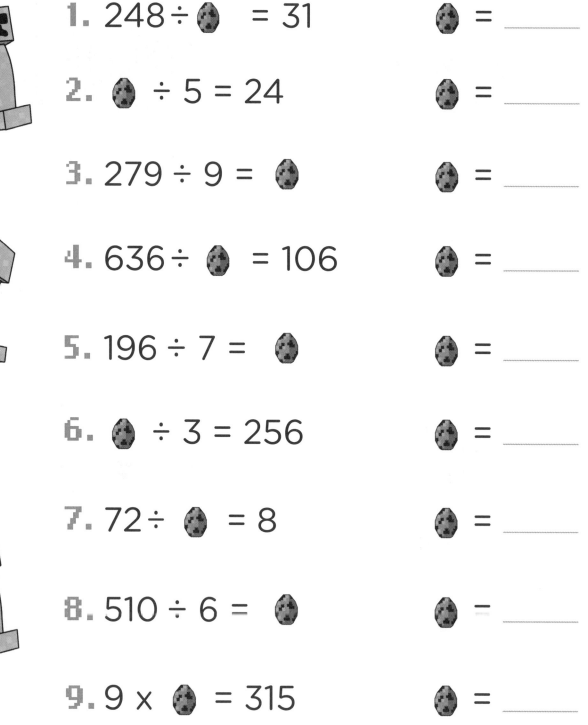 $= 31$ 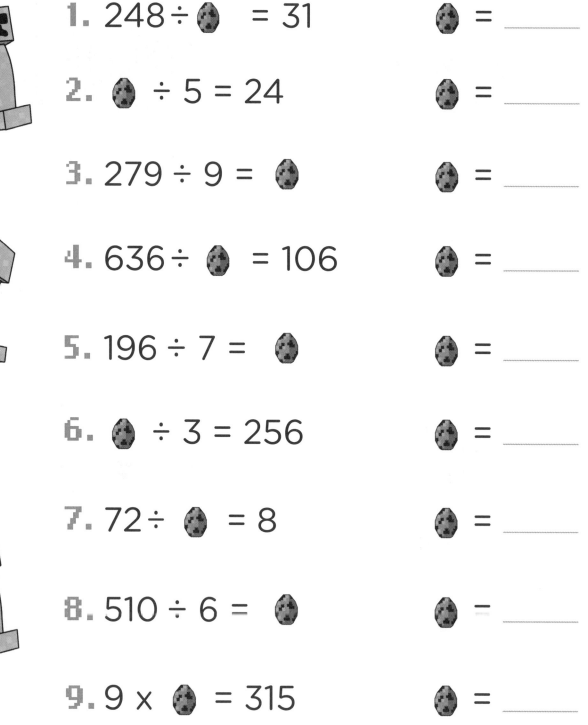 = _____

2. 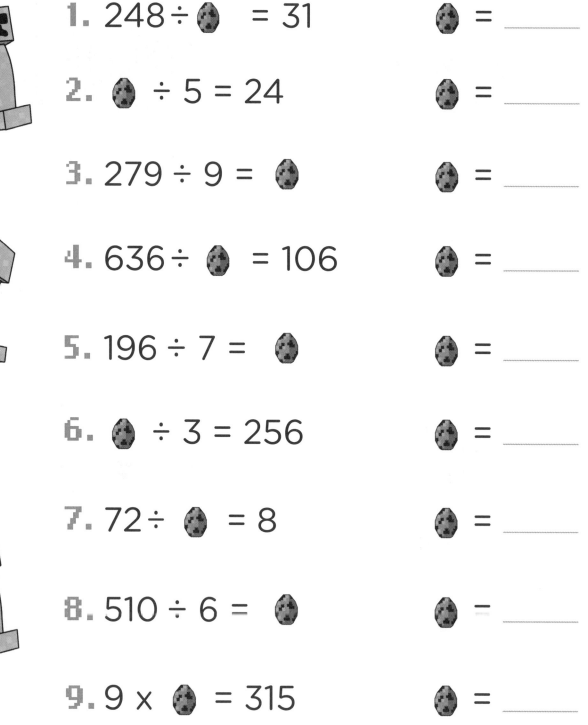 $\div 5 = 24$ 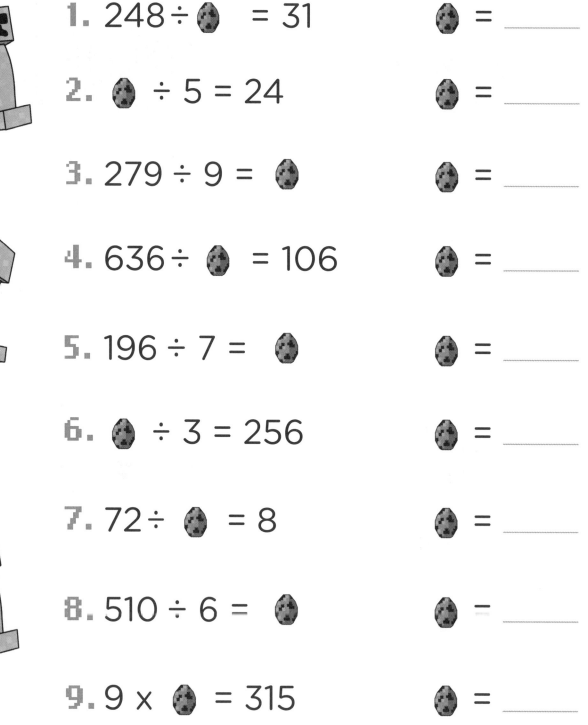 = _____

3. $279 \div 9 =$ 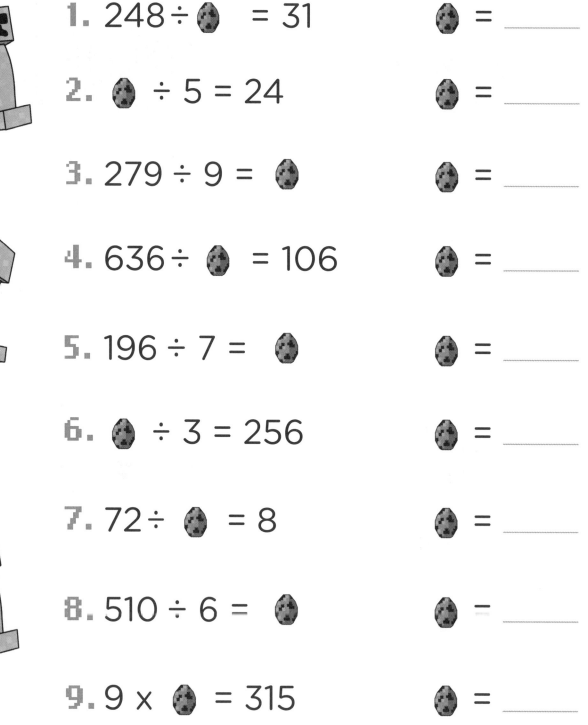   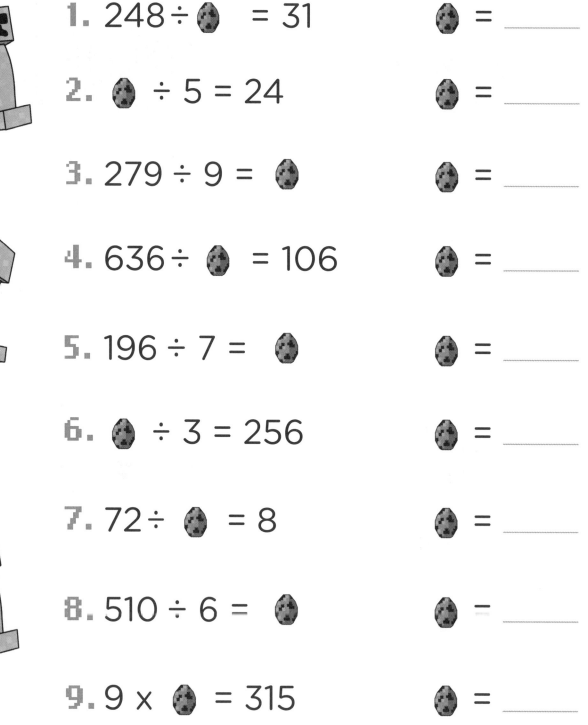 = _____

4. $636 \div$ 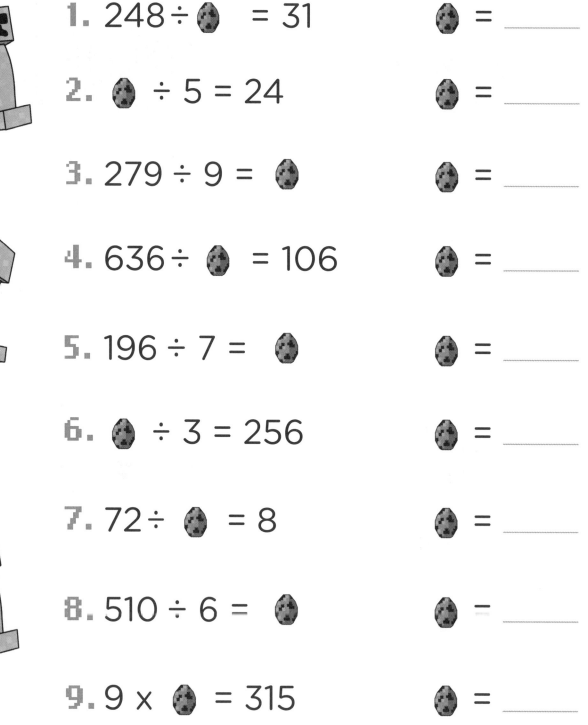 $= 106$ 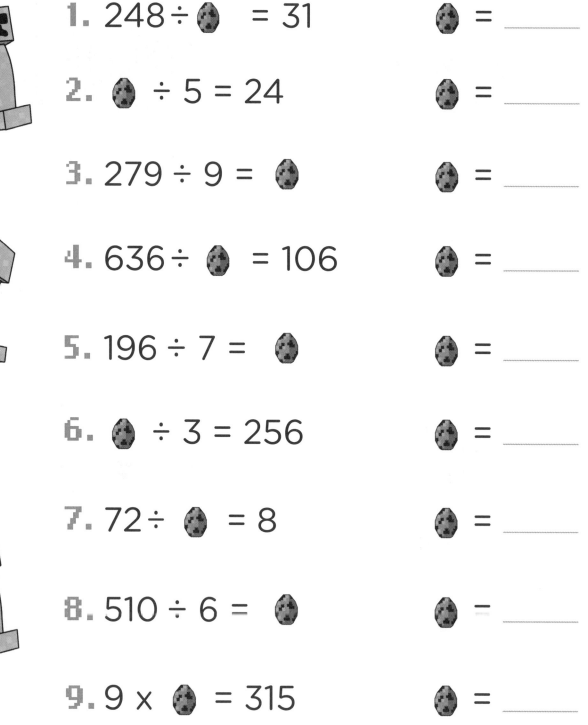 = _____

5. $196 \div 7 =$ 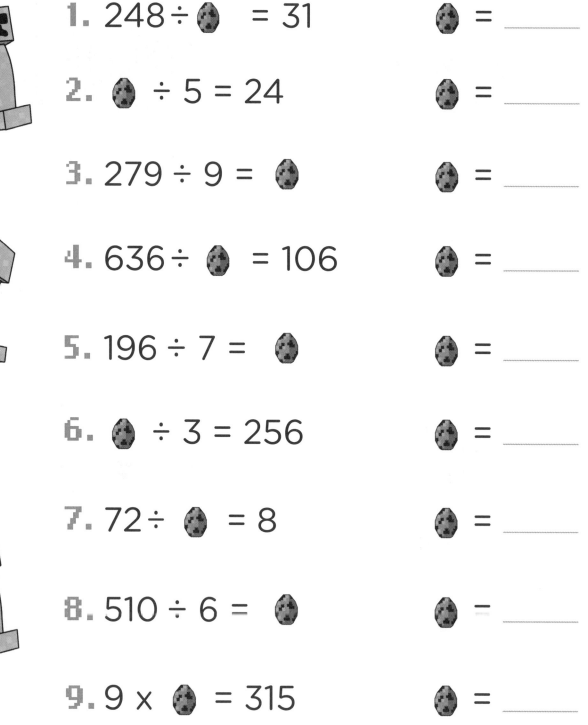   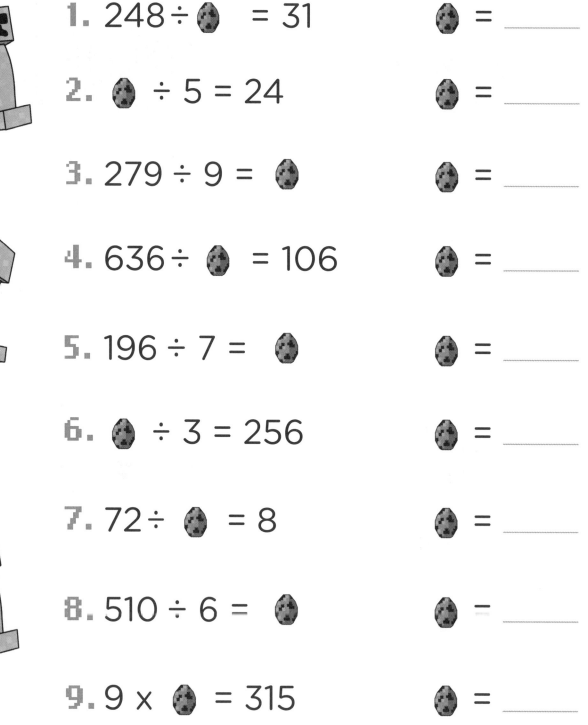 = _____

6. 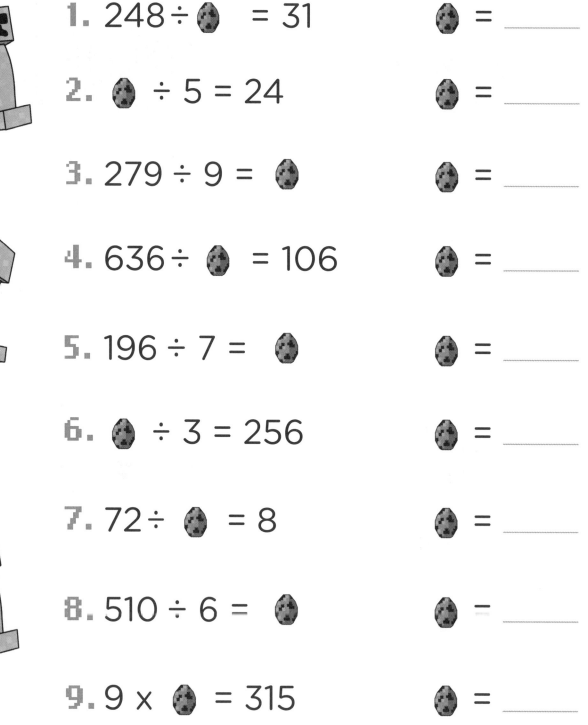 $\div 3 = 256$ 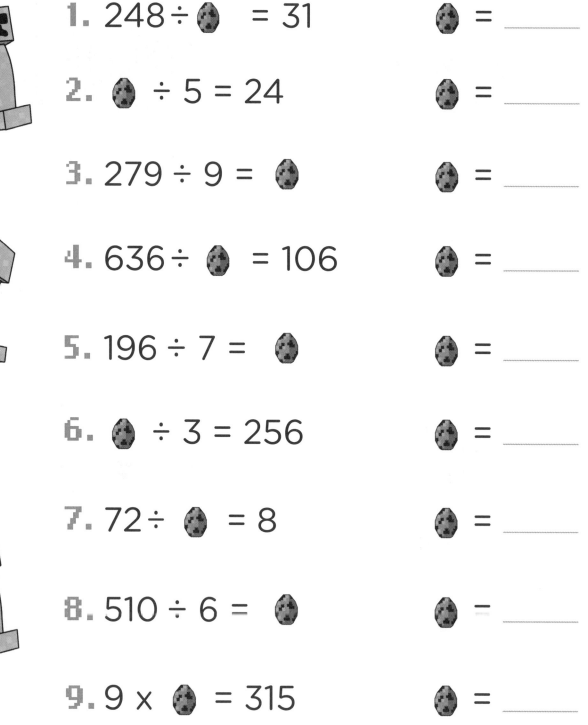 = _____

7. $72 \div$ 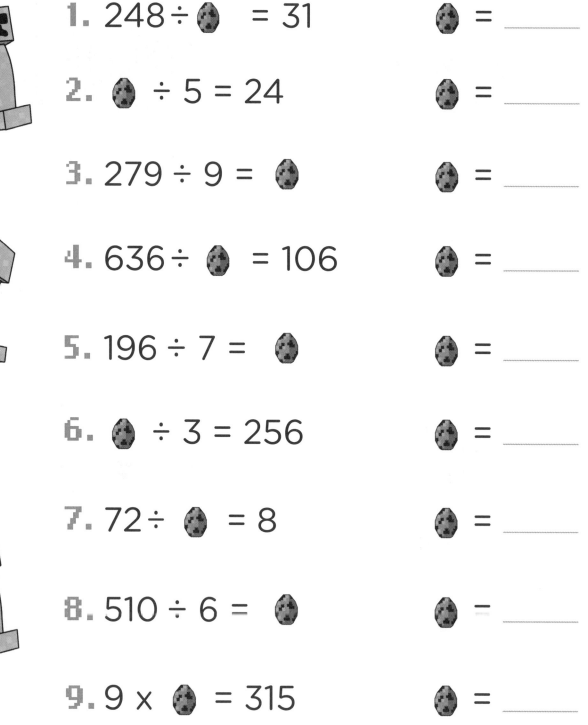 $= 8$ 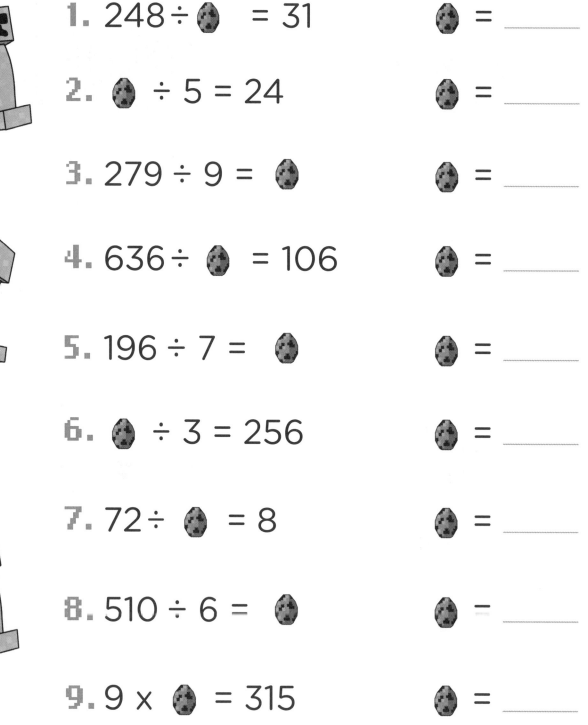 = _____

8. $510 \div 6 =$ 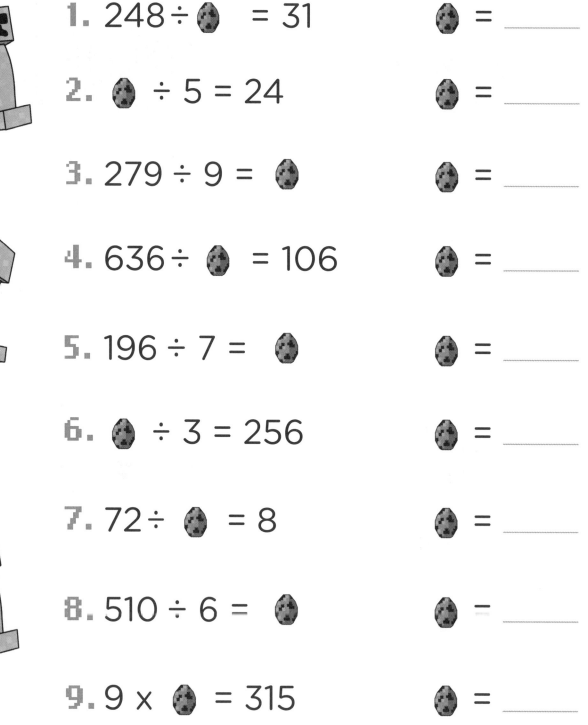   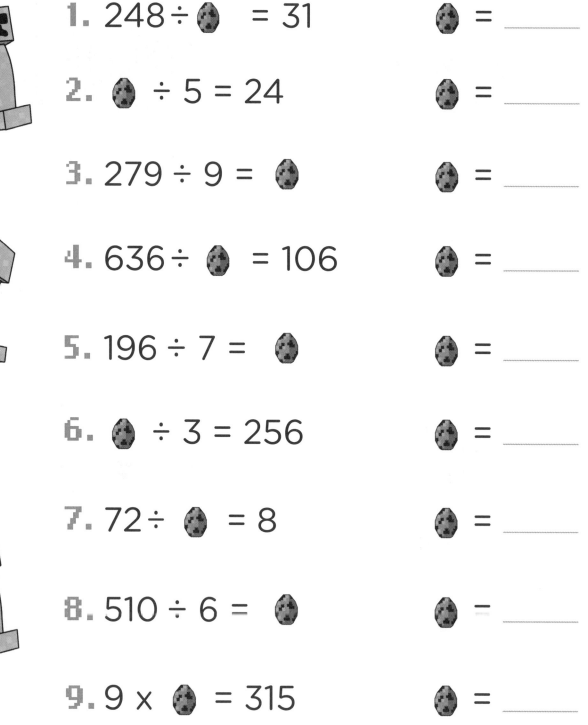 = _____

9. $9 \times$ 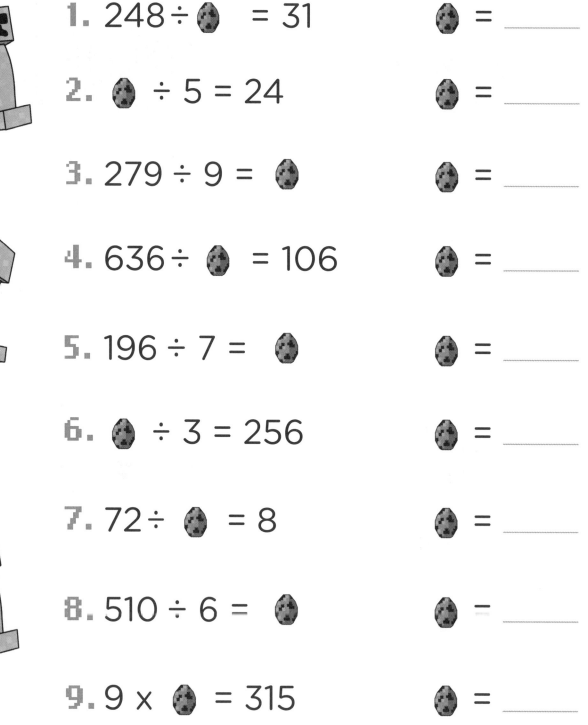 $= 315$ 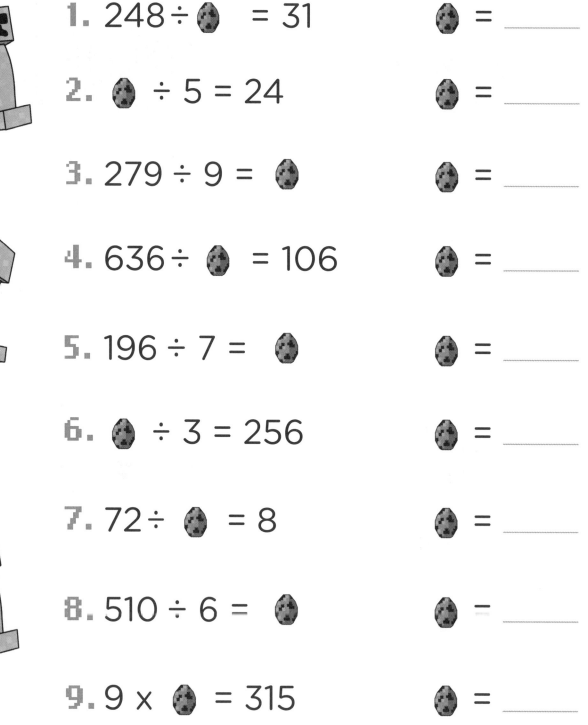 = _____

MYSTERY MESSAGE
WITH MULTIPLICATION AND DIVISION

Solve the multiplication and division problems below. Then write the letters in the blank spaces at the bottom of the page to get the answer to the joke!

1. $624 \div 4 =$ _____ $\underline{I}$

2. $23 \times 7 =$ _____ $\underline{B}$

3. $612 \div 9 =$ _____ $\underline{A}$

4. $546 \div 7 =$ _____ $\underline{R}$

5. $39 \times 5 =$ _____ $\underline{Y}$

6. $124 \times 3 =$ _____ $\underline{L}$

Q: Which building has the most stories?

COPY THE LETTERS FROM THE ANSWERS ABOVE TO FIND OUT.

Answer:

$\overline{68}$ $\overline{372}$ $\overline{156}$ $\overline{161}$ $\overline{78}$ $\overline{68}$ $\overline{78}$ $\overline{195}$

IRON GOLEM'S GUIDE TO PLACE VALUE

Solve the division equations below to fill in the empty place value box beside each one.

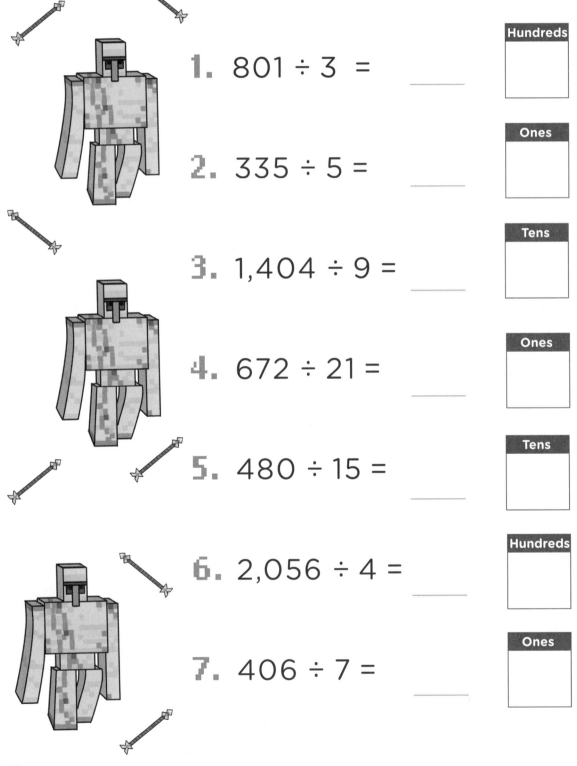

1. 801 ÷ 3 = _____

Hundreds
[ ]

2. 335 ÷ 5 = _____

Ones
[ ]

3. 1,404 ÷ 9 = _____

Tens
[ ]

4. 672 ÷ 21 = _____

Ones
[ ]

5. 480 ÷ 15 = _____

Tens
[ ]

6. 2,056 ÷ 4 = _____

Hundreds
[ ]

7. 406 ÷ 7 = _____

Ones
[ ]

SKIP COUNT CHALLENGE

A zombie in gold armor has discovered you in the forest! Figure out the number pattern and fill in the blanks to complete the path before he can catch you.

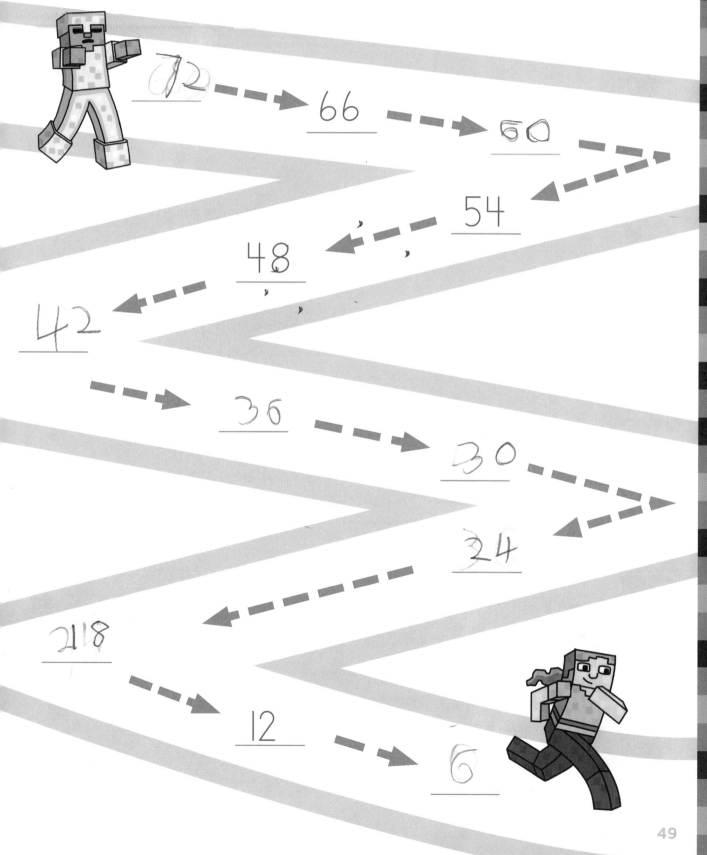

72

66

60

54

48

42

36

30

24

18

12

6

ANIMAL TALLY

Use the six clues below to help you fill in the chart on the right-hand page.

1. If Steve can fit 5 chickens at each of his farms and he has 2 farms full of chickens, plus 3 extra chickens that he keeps in his house, how many chickens total does he have?

2. If Alex has 3 times as many chickens as Steve, how many does she have?

3. If Steve has 46 horses and Alex has ½ the amount that he has, how many horses does she have?

4. If Steve has 18 sheep and Alex has 4 times that number of sheep, how many sheep does she have?

5. If Steve has 7 groups of 12 cows, how many cows does he have?

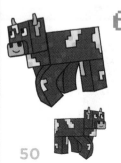

6. If Alex has ⅙ the amount of cows as Steve, how many cows does she have total?

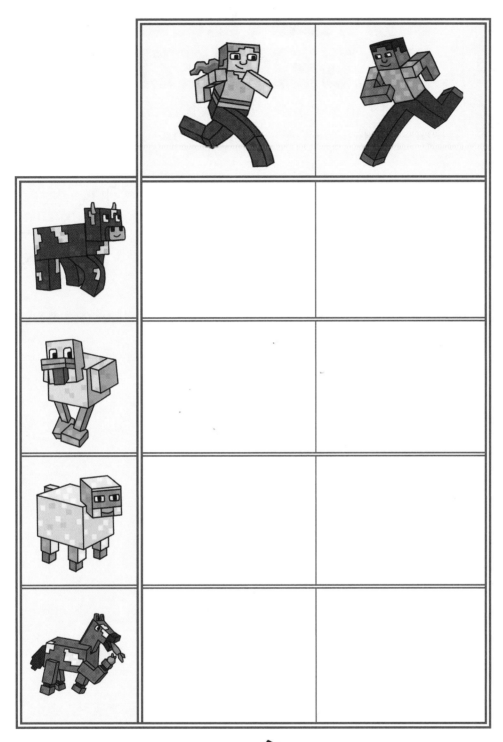

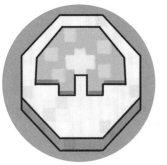

ADVENTURES IN GEOMETRY

Label the red lines on each image as parallel, perpendicular, or intersecting.

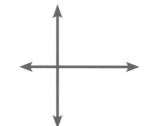

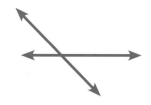

Parallel Lines　　**Perpendicular Lines**　　**Intersecting Lines**

1. perpendicular

2. perpendicular

3. perpendicular

4. <u>parallel</u>

5. <u>parallel</u>

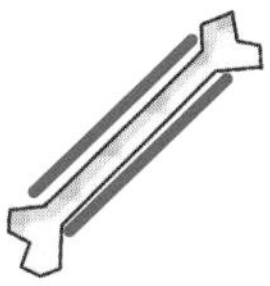

6. <u>parallel</u>

7. <u>perpendicular</u>

WORD PROBLEMS

Use multiplication and division to solve these word problems.

1. Alex's pig will walk 5 feet before eating the dangling carrot. Alex wants her pig to walk 250 feet. How many carrots will she need?

2. Each melon slice has 4 seeds. After Steve cuts up his melon block he has 52 seeds. How many slices were in his melon block?

3. Each shelf in the library holds 10 books. The library has 63 shelves. How many books are there in total?

4. A bee lives in a hive with 120 other bees. A mob of skeletons shake the hive and 1/3 of the bees fly away. How many bees are left?

5. A golden thread that is 6 inches long lets you cast 4 enchantments. If the thread is 54 inches long, how many enchantments can you cast?

6. A torch will light up 7 blocks. You want to get back to your house, which is 490 blocks away. How many torches will you need to light your path?

7. You made 22 pumpkin pies for your friends, and each pie will be cut into 8 slices. A wolf eats 1 slice out of every pie. How many slices do you have left for your friends?

GIANT'S GUIDE TO PLACE VALUE

Answer the multiplication and division questions below. Write the correct digit in the place value box.

1. 568 ÷ 4 = _____

2. 2765 ÷ 7 = _____

3. 19,450 ÷ 10 = _____

4. 456 x 12 = _____

5. 302,576 ÷ 8 = _____

6. 1045 ÷ 5 = _____

7. 389,724 ÷ 3 = _____

Tens

Hundreds

Thousands

Ones

Ten Thousands

Hundreds

Hundred Thousands

EQUAL FRACTIONS

One day in Steve's world is 120 minutes in real life!
Use multiplication and division to fill in the chart
and find out how much time Steve spends on each activity.

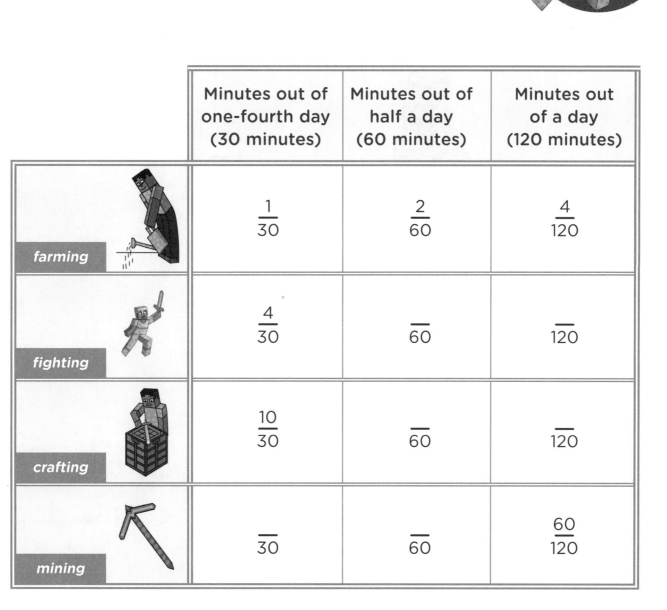

	Minutes out of one-fourth day (30 minutes)	Minutes out of half a day (60 minutes)	Minutes out of a day (120 minutes)
farming	$\frac{1}{30}$	$\frac{2}{60}$	$\frac{4}{120}$
fighting	$\frac{4}{30}$	$\frac{}{60}$	$\frac{}{120}$
crafting	$\frac{10}{30}$	$\frac{}{60}$	$\frac{}{120}$
mining	$\frac{}{30}$	$\frac{}{60}$	$\frac{60}{120}$

What does Steve spend most of his day doing? _____

COMPARING FRACTIONS

Can a skeleton take down a ghast? Compare the fractions and circle the one that is greater to determine who wins in each battle.

HINT: Draw two same-sized boxes and shade them in to help you compare.

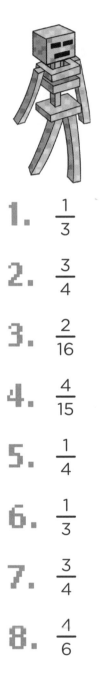

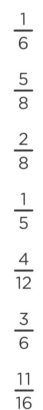

1. $\frac{1}{3}$ $\frac{1}{6}$

2. $\frac{3}{4}$ $\frac{5}{8}$

3. $\frac{2}{16}$ $\frac{2}{8}$

4. $\frac{4}{15}$ $\frac{1}{5}$

5. $\frac{1}{4}$ $\frac{4}{12}$

6. $\frac{1}{3}$ $\frac{3}{6}$

7. $\frac{3}{4}$ $\frac{11}{16}$

8. $\frac{4}{6}$ $\frac{1}{2}$

Who won the most battles overall?

_____

GEOMETRY WORD PROBLEMS

Solve the problems using multiplication and division.

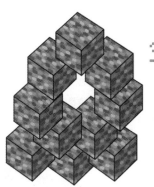

1. If Alex builds a square wall out of lapis lazuli and the wall has an area of 25 square feet, how many feet long is each side of the wall?

2. A Minecrafter's bookcase is shaped like a cube. If each side of that cube is 3 feet long, how many bookcases can you squeeze onto a 144-square-foot floor?

3. Alex has a rectangular fenced-in area that is 5,400 square feet. If the length of the fence is 90 feet, how wide is it?

4. Steve walks the perimeter of his house three times each day to check for zombies and creepers. If all the sides of his house are 16 feet long, how many feet does Steve walk every day?

GEOMETRY WORD PROBLEMS (CONTINUED)

5. Alex's treasure chest measures 10 feet by 8 feet. She can fit 4 emeralds in every square foot. How many emeralds can she fit in the chest?

6. Steve built a rectangular obsidian wall that has a perimeter of 34 feet. If the wall is 7 feet long, how wide is it?

7. Steve wants to fit all 16 of his pet cats inside his house. If each cat needs 4 square feet to move freely, how long do the sides of his square house have to be?

ANSWER KEY

Page 6: Multiplication by Grouping
2. 2 x 8 = 16 swords
3. 4 x 6 = 24 axes
4. 3 x 4 = 12 arrows
5. 5 x 7 = 35 torches

Page 7:
Mystery Message with Multiplication
2. 30
3. 42
4. 72
5. 56
6. 35
7. 18
8. 48
9. 40
Answer: THE GROUND

Page 8: Enderman's Guide to Place Value
2. 1,000 + 500 + 0 + 9
3. 8,000 + 0 + 30 + 4
4. 5,000 + 600 + 10 + 2
5. 2,000 + 900 + 10 + 3
6. 7,000 + 300 + 80 + 9
7. 3,000 + 400 + 90 + 0

Page 9: Math Facts Challenge
6, 12, 18, 24, 30, 36, 42, 48, 54, 60, 66

Page 10: Telling Time
2. 3:15
3. 12:25
4. 7:40
5. 8:45
6. 2:05

Page 11: The Trading Table
1. 14 emeralds
2. 35 emeralds
3. 28 emeralds
4. 42 emeralds
5. The shepherd and the cleric.
6. The fisherman.
7. The tool smith's collection.

Pages 12–13: Geometry Skills Practice
2. 3 x 5 = 15 fishing rods
3. 3 x 9 = 27 carrots
4. 5 x 7 = 35 pumpkin pies
5. 2 x 6 = 12 elytra
6. 4 x 5 = 20 grass blocks
7. 1 x 7 = 7 shears
8. 4 x 2 = 8 bees
9. 4 x 6 = 24 goats
Hardcore Mode: 4 x 7 = 28 + 6 = 34 creepers

Pages 14–15: Multiplication Word Problems
2. 16 diamonds
3. 16 grass blocks
4. 21 buckets of milk
5. 20 eggs
6. 27 wood blocks
7. 15 TNT blocks
8. 7 carrots
9. 18 blocks of snow

Page 16:
Snow Golem's Guide to Place Value
2. 24, 20
3. 9, 10
4. 49, 50
5. 72, 70
6. 56, 60
7. 30, 30

Page 17: Math Facts Challenge
3, 6, 9, 12, 15, 18, 21, 24, 27, 30, 33, 36

Page 18: Minute Hand Mystery

2. 15 minutes 3. 5 minutes

4. 20 minutes 5. 50 minutes

6. 25 minutes

Page 19: Equal Trade

1. 2 nickels

2. 25 pennies

3. 4 nickels

4. 10 dimes

5. 50 pennies

Page 20: Adventures in Geometry

1, 3, 5

Creative Mode:

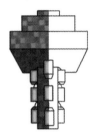

Page 21: Shelter Geometry

1. Area of Alex's wall

    7 x 4 = 28

2. Area of Steve's wall

    5 x 5 = 25

3. Alex's wall

4. 3 more blocks

5. 53

Page 22: Multiplication by Grouping

1. 3 x 4 = 12

2. 5 x 4 = 20

3. 4 x 4 = 16

4. 2 x 4 = 8

5. 6 x 4 = 24

Page 23:
Mystery Message with
Multiplication and Division

2. 108

3. 96

4. 89

5. 744

6. 32

7. 927

8. 31

9. 372

Answer: NEIGH-BORS

Page 24: Ghast's Guide to Place Value

2. C

3. F

4. A

5. D

6. G

7. E

Page 25: Skip Count Challenge

5, 10, 15, 20, 25, 30, 35, 40, 45, 50, 55, 60

Page 26: Telling Time

2. 3:30

3. 6:05

4. 11:20

5. 8:45

6. 10:10

7. 5:35

8. 12:00

Page 27: Spawn Egg Challenge

1. 115

2. 30

3. 282

4. 180

5. 24

6. 78

7. green

8. pink and black

9. 709

Pages 28-29: Equal Parts Challenge

2.

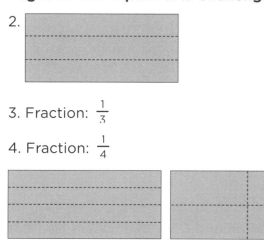

3. Fraction: $\frac{1}{3}$

4. Fraction: $\frac{1}{4}$

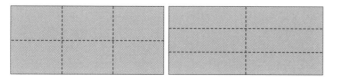

5. Fraction: $\frac{1}{6}$

Page 30: Mystery Message with Multiplication

2. 266
3. 432
4. 162
5. 210
6. 392
7. 133
8. 475
Answer: JIFFY CUBE

Page 31:
Multiplication and Division Mystery Number

2. 24
3. 10
4. 3
5. 6
6. 9
7. 12
8. 4
9. 11
10. 6

Page 32: Ender Dragon's Number Challenge

1. C
2. A
3. E
4. B
5. D

Page 33: Skip Count Challenge

4, 8, 12, 16, 20, 24, 28, 32, 36, 40, 44, 48, 52, 56, 60

Pages 34-35: Creating Potions

1. 8, 4
2. 12. 24
3. 25, 40
4. 21, 42

Fermented Spider Eyes Night Vision Potion

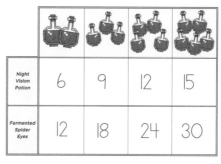

Night Vision Potion	6	9	12	15
Fermented Spider Eyes	12	18	24	30

Pages 36-37:
Adventures in Geometry: Perimeter and Area

1. Current perimeter: 20
New perimeter: 36
2. Current perimeter: 18
New perimeter: 12
3. Current perimeter: 16
New perimeter: 22
4. Current area: 28
New area: 56
5. Current area: 30
New area: 15
6. Current area: 20
New area: 40

Pages 38–39: Word Problems

1. 28 carrots
2. 27 diamonds
3. 24 damage points
4. 5 blocks of iron ore
5. 60 melon pieces
6. 80 arrows
7. 36 bees
8. 18 damage

Page 40: Place Value

1. 168 (B) 2. 624 (C)
3. 294 (G) 4. 350 (A)
5. 420 (F) 6. 495 (D)
7. 832 (E)

Page 41: Squid Number Challenge

1. 180 (F)
2. 103 (D)
3. 228 (A)
4. 738 (B)
5. 336 (G)
6. 294 (C)
7. 91 (E)

Pages 42–43: Mob Measurements

2. 26 inches
3. 41 inches
4. 44 inches
5. 21 inches

Length in meters	Length in cm	Length in mm
1	100	1,000
3	300	3,000
1.5	150	1,500
2.7	270	2,700
2.3	230	2,300

Pages 44–45: Adventures in Geometry

1. obtuse
2. obtuse
3. right
4. obtuse
5. acute
6. right
7. acute
8. obtuse

Page 46:
Multiplication and Division Mystery Number

1. 8
2. 120
3. 31
4. 6
5. 28
6. 768
7. 9
8. 85
9. 35

Page 47:
Mystery Message with Multiplication and Division

1. 156
2. 161
3. 68
4. 78
5. 195
6. 372
Answer: A LIBRARY

Page 48: Iron Golem's Guide to Place Value

1. 267, Hundreds: 2
2. 67, Ones: 7
3. 156, Tens: 5
4. 32, Ones: 2
5. 32, Tens: 3
6. 514, Hundreds: 5
7. 58, Ones: 8

Page 49: Skip Count Challenge

72, 66, 60, 54, 48, 42, 36, 30, 24, 18, 12, 6

Pages 50–51: Animal Tally

1. 13 chickens
2. 39 chickens
3. 23 horses
4. 72 sheep
5. 84 cows
6. 14 cows

	ALEX	STEVE
COWS	14	84
CHICKENS	39	13
SHEEP	72	18
HORSES	23	46

Pages 52–53: Adventures in Geometry

1. Bow and arrow: intersecting
2. experience orb: perpendicular
3. Shears: intersecting
4. Saddle: parallel
5. Tin ingot: parallel
6. Bone: parallel
7. Diamonds: perpendicular

Pages 54–55: Word Problems

1. 50 carrots
2. 13 melon slices
3. 630 books
4. 80 bees
5. 36 enchantments
6. 70 torches
7. 154 slices

Page 56: Giant's Guide to Place Value

1. 142, Tens: 4
2. 395, Hundreds: 3
3. 1,945, Thousands: 1
4. 5,472, Ones: 2
5. 37,822, Ten thousands: 3
6. 209, Hundreds: 2
7. 129,908, Hundred thousands: 1

Page 57: Equal Fractions

Minutes out of one-fourth day (30 minutes)
Minutes out of half a day (60 minutes)
Minutes out of a day (120 minutes)

$\frac{1}{30}$ $\frac{2}{60}$ $\frac{4}{120}$

$\frac{4}{30}$ $\frac{8}{60}$ $\frac{16}{120}$

$\frac{10}{30}$ $\frac{20}{60}$ $\frac{40}{120}$

$\frac{15}{30}$ $\frac{30}{60}$ $\frac{60}{120}$

Answer: Mining

Page 58: Comparing Fractions

1. $\frac{1}{3}$ is greater, skeleton wins
2. $\frac{3}{4}$ is greater, skeleton wins
3. $\frac{2}{8}$ is greater, ghast wins
4. $\frac{4}{15}$ is greater, skeleton wins
5. $\frac{4}{12}$ is greater, ghast wins
6. $\frac{3}{6}$ is greater, ghast wins
7. $\frac{3}{4}$ is greater, skeleton wins
8. $\frac{4}{6}$ is greater, skeleton wins

Skeleton won the most battles overall.

Pages 59–60: Geometry Word Problems

1. 5 feet long
2. 16 bookcases
3. 60 feet wide
4. 192 feet
5. 320 emeralds
6. 10 feet
7. 8 feet

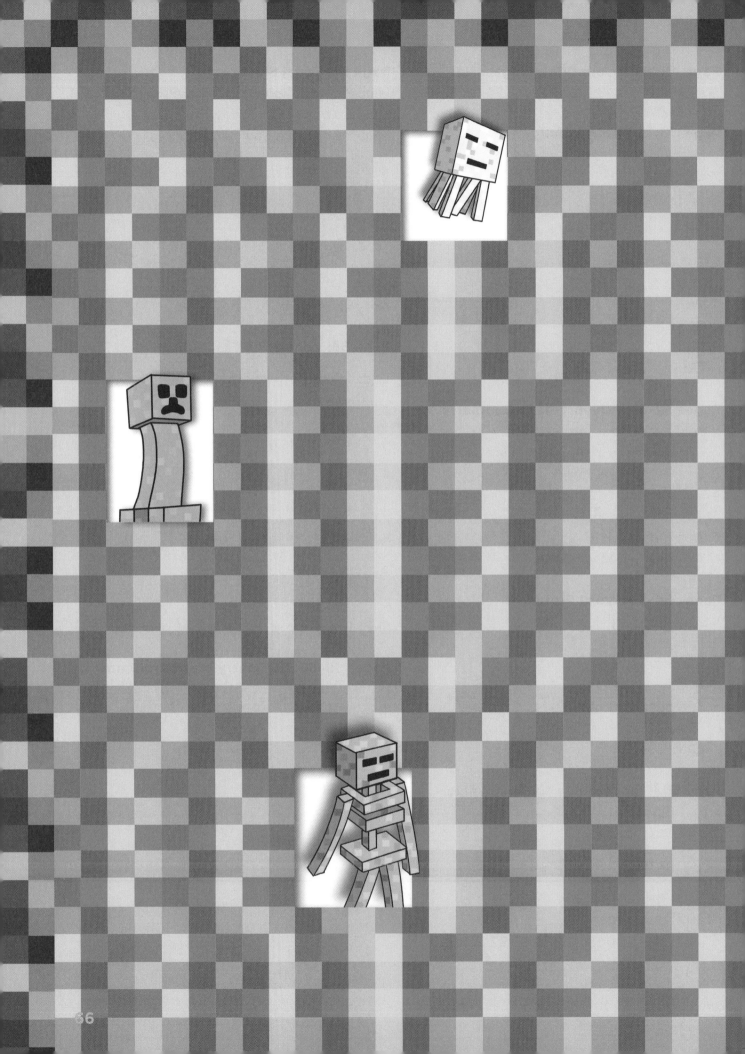

CHAPTER TWO

SPELLING SURVIVAL SKILLS

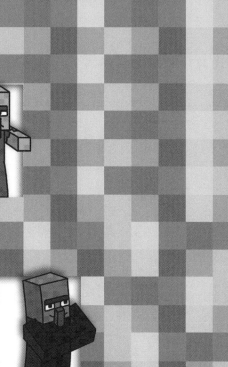

WORD FILL-IN

*Use the box of words to finish the sentences below. (Don't forget to capitalize at the beginning of sentences!) Then circle **long** or **short** to describe the sound the vowel makes.*

safe	best	keep	stand	next

1. You need more XP to reach the   **LONG**   **SHORT**

_____ level.

2. _____ an eye out for mineshafts   **LONG**   **SHORT**

when you're traveling in the ocean.

3. To help your horses stay _____,   **LONG**   **SHORT**

leash them to a fencepost.

4. You can _____ on a block so it's   **LONG**   **SHORT**

easier to see.

5. The _____ way to kill spiders is   **LONG**   **SHORT**

with a bow and arrow at a distance.

STEVE'S WORD SCRAMBLE

*Unscramble the words below, and write them correctly on the line. Then circle **long** or **short** to describe the sound the vowel makes.*

dress	grade	plant	save	reach

1. For the most protection, **sdres** _____ in diamond armor.   LONG   SHORT

2. Enchanting books can help you **esva** _____ enchants to apply later.   LONG   SHORT

3. If you find pumpkin seeds, **ntalp** _____ them.   LONG   SHORT

4. To **arhec** _____ higher, use a ladder.   LONG   SHORT

5. Don't you wish you could get a **agerd** _____ for playing Minecraft?   LONG   SHORT

ORDER CHALLENGE

*Practice spelling the sight words below as you write them on the lines in **alphabetical order** from top to bottom.*

every	high	near	between	own	easy

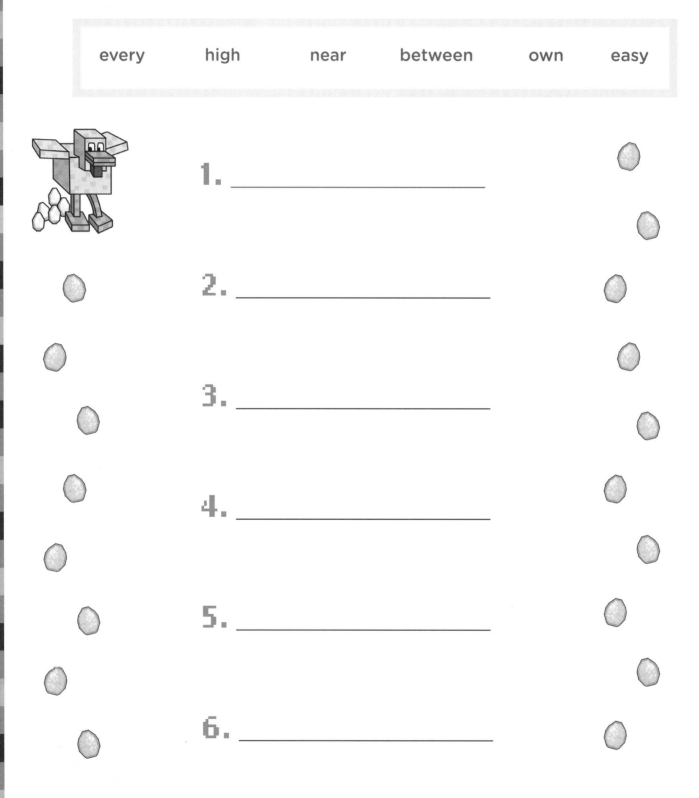

1. _____

2. _____

3. _____

4. _____

5. _____

6. _____

FIND AND FIX

Look for one spelling mistake in each sentence below. Cross out the mistake and write the word correctly on the line.

1. It is very easie to get lost in the Nether. _____

2. In a Flower Forest Biome, you'll find almost evary type of flower. _____

3. To keep hostile mobs from spawning nere your home, light up the area. _____

4. You can create your oyn skin in Minecraft. _____

5. The Ender Dragon flies betwine special obsidian columns. _____

6. Wither skeletons are taller than regular skeletons at two and a half blocks hi instead of two. _____

71

DEAR ALEX

Write a short letter to Alex telling her about your latest Minecraft adventure. Your challenge: use as many of the sight words below as you can.

every	high	near	between	own	easy

Dear Alex,

_____

_____

_____

_____

_____

_____

_____

Sincerely,

_____

WITHER'S WORD SEARCH

Can you find and circle all the words from the list?

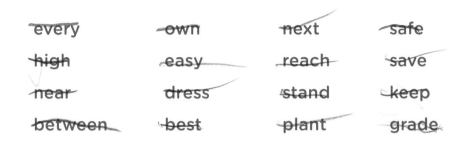

every	own	next	safe
high	easy	reach	save
near	dress	stand	keep
between	best	plant	grade

```
S T V D H R B O Z P Y Z
A Z S I R E E D W T T Q
F J G E T E G A R N Z N
E H A W B R S R C J N N
T S E L Y S B S A H R D
Y E D R L T V W N D X L
N T E D Y A V D P T E V
P V X N T N X L N E A R
E E T E K D A Y V T L J
Z T E M N N X A L Y Q J
B B X K T M S L D R L Z
```

73

WORD FILL-IN

*Use the box of words to finish the sentences below. Then circle **long** or **short** to describe the sound the vowel makes.*

slip	cute	groan	stop	ride

1. Baby zombies are _____ but very deadly! LONG SHORT

2. You can build so many things in Minecraft, even a _____ 'n' slide for water fun. LONG SHORT

3. When villagers get tired of trading something with you, they may _____ accepting it. LONG SHORT

4. You can hear a zombie _____ from 16 blocks away. LONG SHORT

5. It looks like fun to _____ in a minecart. LONG SHORT

STEVE'S WORD SCRAMBLE

Unscramble the words below, and write them correctly on the line. Then circle long or short to describe the sound the vowel makes.

1. To find a Nether fortress, look for straight edges, **LONG   SHORT**

   instead of jagged **kroc** _____ edges you

   see in netherrack cliffs and mountains.

2. The music in Minecraft is not meant for you to **LONG   SHORT**

   nsgi _____ along.

3. I **ehop** _____ I can beat the Ender **LONG   SHORT**

   Dragon.

4. Magma cubes attack by trying to **LONG   SHORT**

   mujp_____ on top of you.

5. You may find squid when you **dvie** **LONG   SHORT**

   _____ into the water.

RAINBOW WRITING

Practice spelling the sight words below. First, write each word in pencil. Then trace over the letters three times with a different color of crayon each time.

always	thought	start	city	school	front

1. _____

2. _____

3. _____

4. _____

5. _____

6. _____

WORD BUDDIES

Write two sight words that share a letter and criss-cross them at that letter. Make three pairs of word buddies to include all of the sight words below.

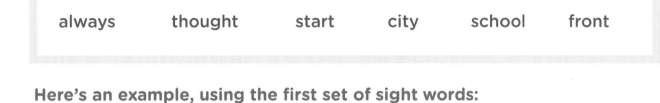

| always | thought | start | city | school | front |

Here's an example, using the first set of sight words:

```
        n
  e v e r y
        a
        r
```

1. *Word Buddies: Pair 1*

2. *Word Buddies: Pair 2*

3. *Word Buddies: Pair 3*

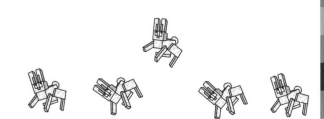

RHYME BLOCKS

Write the spelling words on the left column lines. Then write a word that rhymes with each on the right.

jump	rock	start	thought	school	ride

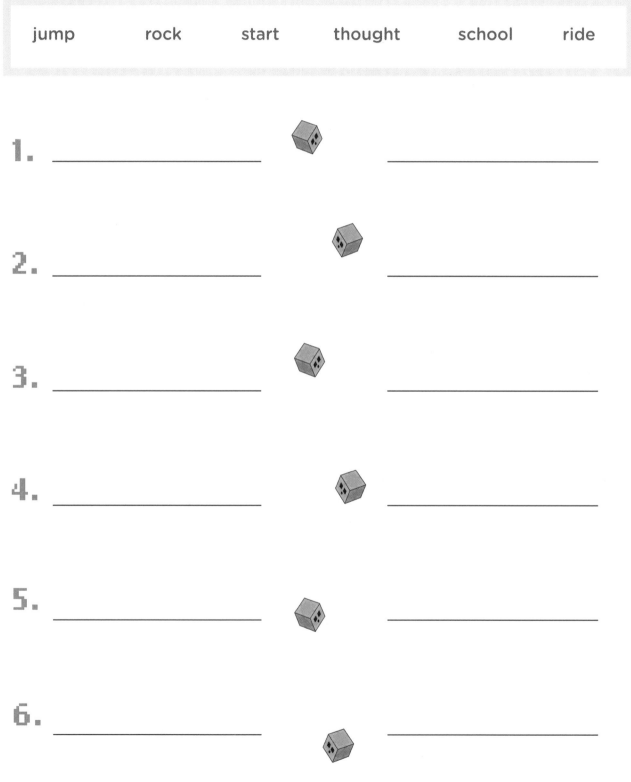

1. _____   _____

2. _____   _____

3. _____   _____

4. _____   _____

5. _____   _____

6. _____   _____

WITHER'S WORD SEARCH

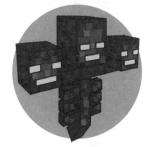

Can you find and circle all the words from the list?

always	~~school~~	sing	cute
~~thought~~	front	stop	groan
start	slip	rock	dive
city	jump	hope	ride

```
P R I D E E T G S R
M L W V A H P T L V
U C I G O L A O R Z
J D U U R R W N H S
G L G T T O Y A L R
F H O S E T A I Y S
T R I O I R P N T S
V N O C H O M O K R
G X T N M C P Q B T
D Q Z R T K S P P G
```

END BLENDS

*Use the box of **end blend** choices to complete the words in the sentences.*

| gh | tch | ch | sh | th |

1. Villagers will breed only if there are enou __gh__ doors in the village.

2. Cold Bea __ch__ is a snowy biome.

3. Wa __tch__ out for chicken jockeys!

4. A spider jockey has the strength of bo __th__ spider and skeleton mobs.

5. Alex's minecrart is about to cra __sh__ into a wall!

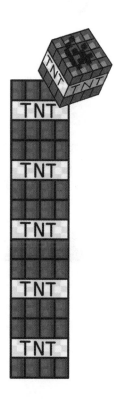

DEAR ALEX

Write a short letter to Alex telling her about the events of your past week. Your challenge: use as many of the end blend words below as you can.

| graph | photograph | laugh | match | push |

Dear Alex,

_____

_____

_____

_____

_____

_____

_____

Sincerely,

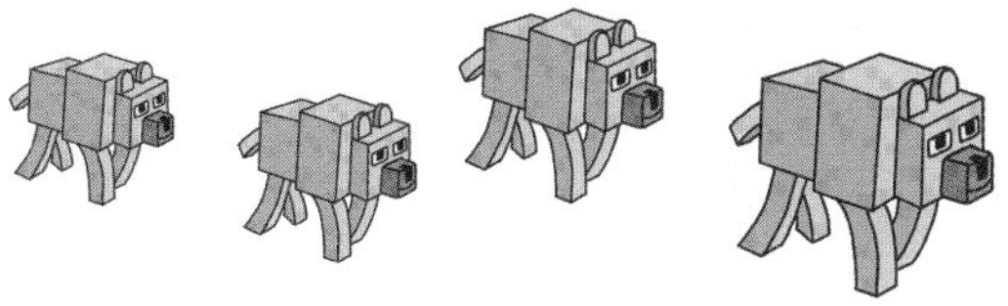

_____

GROWING WORDS

Practice spelling the sight words. Start with the word with the fewest letters, writing the words on the lines in order **from smallest to biggest word.** *If two words have the same number of letters, put them in alphabetical order.*

area	zero	nothing	anything	something	close

1. _____

2. _____

3. _____

4. _____

5. _____

6. _____

FIND AND FIX

Look for one spelling mistake in each sentence below. Cross out the mistake and write the word correctly on the line. Be sure to use capital letters at the start of sentences.

1. Nuthing is better than making a new discovery in Minecraft.

   _____

2. I learn sumthing new every time I play.

   _____

3. Use TNT to blast out a large areya.

   _____

4. You can build just about anithing you can imagine.

   _____

5. When an Ender Dragon is closs by, its purple health bar

   appears on your screen.

   _____

6. You need to eat when your hunger bar gets to ziro.

   _____

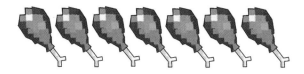

WORD BUDDIES

Write two sight words that share a letter and criss-cross them at that letter. Make three pairs of word buddies to include all of the sight words below.

area	zero	nothing	anything	something	close

Here's an example, using the first set of sight words:

n
every
a
r

1. *Word Buddies: Pair 1*

2. *Word Buddies: Pair 2*

3. *Word Buddies: Pair 3*

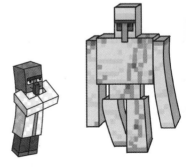

WITHER'S WORD SEARCH

Can you find and circle all the words from the list?

area	something	photograph	beach
zero	close	laugh	crash
nothing	enough	match	push
anything	graph	watch	both

```
Z K N K G D Q D M X B L P
E K T A E N H G U O N E H
R Y D S N T I B L D D C R
O H O G O Y Y H G T A Q J
Y L P B R Q T N T E M G Y
C A Y A W A I H B O M L B
M U H Y R H P X I A N L M
D G Z S T G L H T N P Z L
A H P E A Y O C B H G X D
G E M U R R H T C T Y T B
X O R Q S N C T O D P N B
S B P A M H A N D H R Y Q
K B G L D W X B D V P K L
```

SOFT SOUNDS

Circle the correct letter to complete the words in the sentences.

1. Fen___e in iron golems to stop them from wandering away.

c *or* **s ?**

2. Don't be ___entle with a creeper!

j *or* **g ?**

3. Some Minecrafters have made a giant pen___il in the game.

c *or* **s ?**

4. You can power an en___ine with redstone in BuildCraft.

j *or* **g ?**

5. Leave one block of spa___e between each bookshelf and the enchantment table.

c *or* **s ?**

DEAR ALEX

Write a short letter to Alex telling her what crazy additions you would make in new editions of Minecraft. Your challenge: use as many of the **soft C and G words** below as you can.

price	police	dance	giraffe	stage

Dear Alex,

_____

_____

_____

_____

_____

_____

_____

_____

Sincerely,

_____

RAINBOW WRITING

Practice spelling the sight words below. First, write each word in pencil. Then trace over the letters three times with a different color of crayon each time.

love	can't	cannot	let's	important	begin

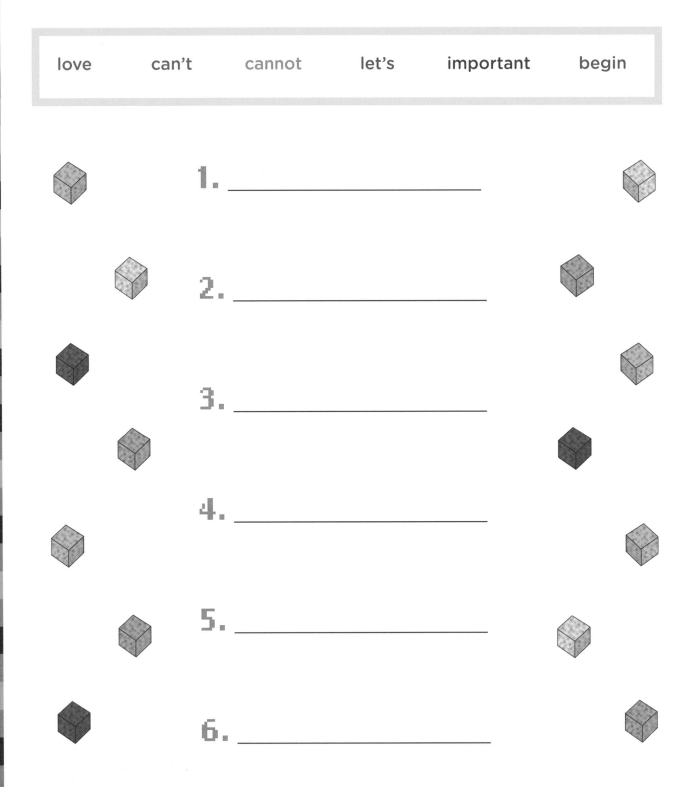

1. _____

2. _____

3. _____

4. _____

5. _____

6. _____

STEVE'S WORD SCRAMBLE

*Unscramble the words below, and write them correctly on the line. (Hint: Choose from the sight words on page 88.) Then circle **how many syllables** they contain.*

1. Are you ready to **giben** _____ a Minecraft journey?

SYLLABLES: **1** or **2**?

2. Desert temples are a good source for rare loot you **nac't** _____ find anywhere else.

SYLLABLES: **1** or **2**?

3. It is **imortiptan** _____ to keep eating during battles.

SYLLABLES: **2** or **3**?

4. Villagers in **ovle** _____ mode produce hearts and a baby villager.

SYLLABLES: **1** or **2**?

5. Wither skeletons **natcon** _____ pass through two-high spaces.

SYLLABLES: **1** or **2**?

WORD BUDDIES

Write two sight words that share a letter and criss-cross them at that letter. Make three pairs of word buddies to include all of the sight words below.

love   can't   cannot   let's   important   begin

Here's an example, using the first set of sight words:

```
      n
 e v e r y
      a
      r
```

1. *Word Buddies: Pair 1*

2. *Word Buddies: Pair 2*

3. *Word Buddies: Pair 3*

WITHER'S WORD SEARCH

Can you find and circle all the words from the list?

love	important	police	gentle
can't	begin	dance	giraffe
cannot	fence	space	stage
let's	price	pencil	engine

Y N M B P Y L W W E Y Y N X
L L D D R R J J E R C E T T
E T D J M Y Y B K N C N B B
T T T L I C N E P A I E A N
' L Y O I Z D Y P J C G I D
S B P D N M T S N I P G N K
C P D M E N P Y L N E G E E
P A B C R B A O Z B I G V M
G E N T L E P C R R A O D K
Q E P ' D N Y K A T L N T P
F M R D T T Y F S M A Y T B
M T I V Y L F D N M T N R M
J Y C X B E N R N B L Q T Q
V N E K W P R N B N T T P Q

GLIDING VOWELS

*A **gliding vowel** (also called a **diphthong**) is a combination of two adjacent vowel sounds in the same syllable. Use the box of choices to complete the words in the sentences.*

| oi | oy | ou | ow |

1. Do you hear a n_oi_se in the cave?

2. Creepers can ann_oy_ you very easily.

3. Dig into a m_ou_ntain and close it up for a quick shelter.

4. Cocoa beans make br_ow_n dye.

5. Guardians are underwater fish-like mobs that spawn

ar_ou_nd an ocean monument.

DEAR ALEX

*Write a short letter to Alex sharing the details of a Minecraft tournament in which you are a player. Your challenge: use as many of the words with **gliding vowels (diphthongs)** below as you can.*

| choice | ground | crown | shout | mouth |

Dear Alex,

_____

_____

_____

_____

_____

_____

_____

Sincerely,

_____

ORDER CHALLENGE

*Practice spelling the sight words below as you write them on the lines in **alphabetical order** from top to bottom.*

today   yesterday   together   child   children   idea

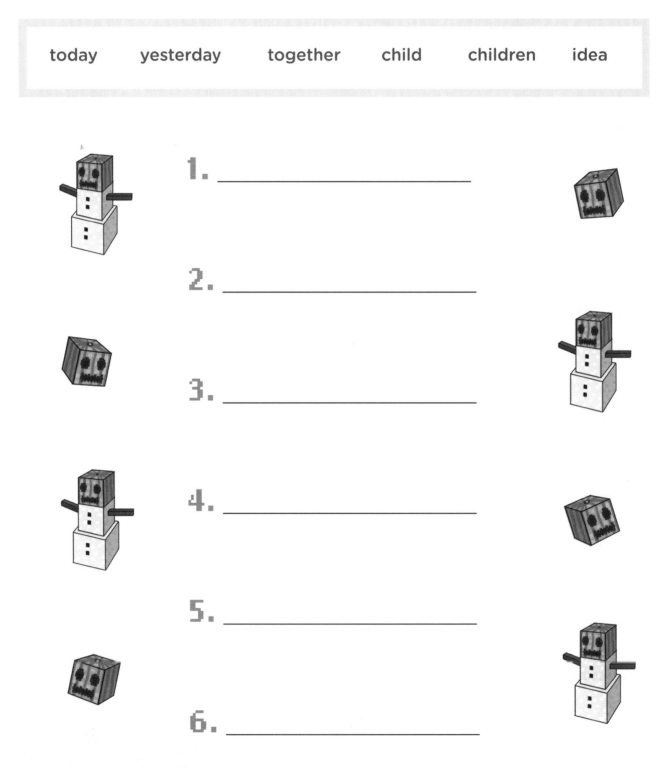

1. _____

2. _____

3. _____

4. _____

5. _____

6. _____

RAINBOW WRITING

Practice spelling the sight words below. First, write each word in pencil. Then trace over the letters three times with a different color of crayon each time.

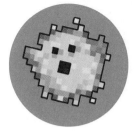

| today | yesterday | together | child | children | idea |

1. _____

2. _____

3. _____

4. _____

5. _____

6. _____

FIND AND FIX

Look for one spelling mistake in each sentence below. Cross out the mistake and write the word correctly on the line.

1. Ghasts make a noyse that sounds like a cat. _____

2. Playing Minecraft tagether is fun. _____

3. An Enderman will open its mowth and _____

shake when provoked.

4. I built a roller coaster in Minecraft taday. _____

5. Villagers with broun robes will tend to _____

nearby crops.

6. It's a good idia to repair your weapons _____

and tools before they break.

WITHER'S WORD SEARCH

Can you find and circle all the words from the list?

today	children	annoy	shout
yesterday	idea	ground	mouth
together	choice	around	mountain
child	noise	crown	brown

```
M J M M L N A L K D N Z N L K
R J T L N J B E M J B M Z J D
N Y R N Z G R Y D C H I L D J
R E H T E G O T A I J Y B L T
N E R D L I H C J D A J R M G
M X B N N J Y T B D O N L Z E
B O K L P U L D R Z G T N C M
R D U L N N O E P R X T I O R
O N T N Q W T R O Y U O U V Y
W T O R T S O U A O H T L M Y
N L Y I E A N R H C H N Y V T
M W J Y S D I S C G Y L L X K
Q L Z D N E Y N D Y T Q K R V
```

WHICH IS IT?

*These **homophones** sound alike but do not fit into the sentence meaning in the same way. Circle the one that makes sense to fill in the blank.*

1. Build your farm _____ .

    hear *or* (here?)

2. A map can help you find

    the ____WAY____ .

    (way) *or* weigh ?

3. I never get ____bored____

    playing Minecraft.

    (bored) *or* board ?

4. You can find a polar ____bear____

    in an icy biome.

    bare *or* (bear?)

5. The yellow ____flower____

    is pretty.

    (flower) *or* flour ?

RHYME BLOCKS

*Write the **homophone** pairs on the left column lines. Then write a word that rhymes with them on the right.*

here/hear   way/weigh   bored/board   bare/bear   flower/flour

1. _____ _____   _____

2. _____ _____   _____

3. _____ _____   _____

4. _____ _____   _____

5. _____ _____   _____

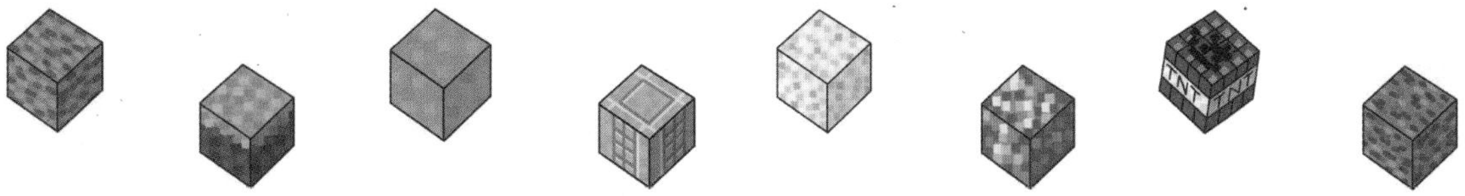

GROWING WORDS

*Practice spelling the sight words. Start with the word with the fewest letters, writing the words on the lines in order **from smallest to biggest word**. If two words have the same number of letters, put them in alphabetical order.*

young	being	sometimes	copy	without	perfect

1. _____

2. _____

3. _____

4. _____

5. _____

6. _____

STEVE'S WORD SCRAMBLE

Unscramble the words below, and write them correctly on the line. (I lint: Choose from the sight words on page 100.) Then circle **how many syllables** *they contain.*

1. Enderman will **mmtiessoe** _____

drop Ender pearls when they die.

SYLLABLES: **2** or **3**?

2. Creative mode is **frecpet** _____ for

building large structures.

SYLLABLES: **1** or **2**?

3. When lava touches flowing water, it creates

cobblestone, **htwiout** _____ using up

any lava or water.

SYLLABLES: **2** or **3**?

4. The closer the moon is to **geinb** _____

a full moon, the more likely it is that zombies

will break down your door.

SYLLABLES: **1** or **2**?

5. You can make a **ugoyn** _____ wolf

grow up faster by feeding it meat.

SYLLABLES: **1** or **2**?

WORD BUDDIES

Write two sight words that share a letter and criss-cross them at that letter. Make three pairs of word buddies to include all of the sight words below.

| young | being | sometimes | copy | without | perfect |

Here's an example, using the first set of sight words:

```
      n
 e v e r y
      a
      r
```

1. *Word Buddies: Pair 1*

2. *Word Buddies: Pair 2*

3. *Word Buddies: Pair 3*

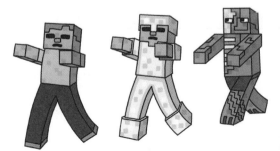

WITHER'S WORD SEARCH

Can you find and circle all the words from the list?

young	without	way	bare
being	perfect	weigh	bear
sometimes	here	bored	flower
copy	hear	board	flour

W T D Q Y E Y R S J L J
I G C A R O L E B E A R
T N W E U Y M O F D N L
H I H N F I A L R T N J
O E G Y T R O W B P J D
U B P E D W E O M T J N
T O M N E I R P R A E H
C O K R G E F L O U R X
S Y J H D B A R E G X L

SEEING DOUBLE

*What **double consonants** are missing from each word? Fill in the blanks to complete the words in the sentences. Use the picture clues to help.*

1. A young dog is called a pu_ll_ _p_y.

2. Steve and Alex must be talking about something fu_n_ _n_y.

3. Use a donkey equipped with a chest to ca_r_ _r_ y your stuff around.

4. Steve looks ha_p_ _p_ y.

5. Each potion is a di_f_ _f_ erent color.

FIND AND FIX

Look for one spelling mistake in each sentence below. Cross out the mistake and write the word correctly on the line.

1. Most potions start with a water botle and
   Nether wart.

   _____

2. There is not just one corect way to
   play Minecraft.

   _____

3. My teacher taught a leson using Minecraft.

   _____

4. Zombies are the most comon hostile mob
   in Minecraft.

   _____

5. You can colect dropped items while on
   a horse.

   _____

RAINBOW WRITING

Practice spelling the sight words below. First, write each word in pencil. Then trace over the letters three times with a different color of crayon each time.

| fly | food | off | took | talk | list |

1. _____

2. _____

3. _____

4. _____

5. _____

6. _____

DEAR ALEX

Write a short letter to Alex telling her about your latest adventure—in Minecraft or in real life. Your challenge: use as many of the sight words below as you can.

| fly | food | off | took | talk | list |

Dear Alex,

_____

_____

_____

_____

_____

_____

_____

Sincerely,

_____

ORDER CHALLENGE

*Practice spelling the sight words below as you write them on the lines in **alphabetical order** from top to bottom.*

| fly | food | off | took | talk | list |

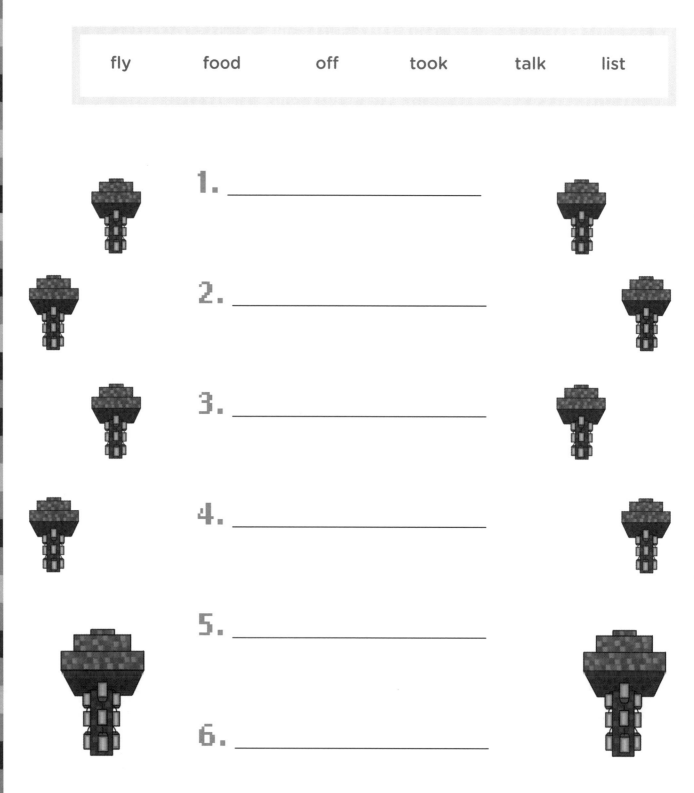

1. _____

2. _____

3. _____

4. _____

5. _____

6. _____

WITHER'S WORD SEARCH

Can you find and circle all the words from the list?

fly	talk	puppy	different
food	list	happy	collect
off	correct	bottle	common
took	funny	lesson	carry

```
C O R R E C T K Y T
B T S I L Y G Y N Y
O N C K V T N E L Y
T O J E A P R N H F
T S C L L E U A U Y
L S K O F L P P R F
E E F F M P O R P K
R L I O Y M A C O Y
G D F F O C O O M N
G Q N G X D T N L D
```

BUILDING COMPOUNDS

*What part is missing from each **compound word**? Fill in the blanks to complete the word. Use the picture clues to help.*

1. The period between daytime and nighttime

is _S_ _U_ _N_ set.

2. Disable the effects by placing a torch on

the side of the _b_ _o_ _o_ _k_ shelf facing the

enchantment table.

3. Do you think playing Minecraft is more fun

than playing _f_ _o_ _o_ _t_ ball?

4. You can make rain _b_ _o_ _w_ sheep that

change colors.

5. You can fish in a _w_ _a_ _t_ _e_ _r_ fall.

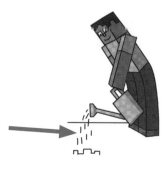

WORD BUDDIES

Write two **compound words** that share a letter and criss-cross them at that letter. Make three pairs of word buddies to include all of the compound words below.

notebook	classroom	everyone
outdoors	sunshine	waterfall

Here's an example, using the first set of sight words:

```
         n
  e v e r y
         a
         r
```

1. *Word Buddies: Pair 1*

2. *Word Buddies: Pair 2*

3. *Word Buddies: Pair 3*

GROWING WORDS

*Practice spelling the sight words. Start with the word with the fewest letters, writing the words on the lines in order **from smallest to biggest word**. If two words have the same number of letters, put them in alphabetical order.*

quiet	visit	almost	buy	once	water

1. _____

2. _____

3. _____

4. _____

5. _____

6. _____

FIND AND FIX

Look for one spelling mistake in each sentence below. Cross out the mistake and write the word correctly on the line. Be sure to use capital letters at the start of sentences.

1. An iron golem's attack is allmost as powerful as a creeper's explosion. _____

2. Watch out when creepers come to viset! _____

3. The music in Minecraft is very quite. _____

4. Onse hostile mobs spawn, they walk around randomly for several seconds. _____

5. Obsidian is created when running watter hits a lava source. _____

6. You can bie melons and pumpkins from villagers. _____

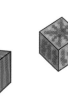

WITHER'S WORD SEARCH

Can you find and circle all the words from the list?

buy	once	bookshelf	sunshine
quiet	water	everyone	rainbow
visit	notebook	outdoors	sunset
almost	classroom	football	waterfall

```
F L E H S K O O B O N C E
W V N S R O O D T U O T G
M A M O D T T T E P E G R
F B T O T S I V Y S W M N
W O D E O E E S N T S M X
O D O M R R B U I U L Y W
B K L T Y F S O N V T M B
N A J O B T A S O W Z M T
I R N R E A H L A K Z R M
A E B I Y I L T L L D B G
R T U U N L E L Q R C D J
N Q L E Y R N R W L B R T
```

SIGHT WORD REVIEW: COPY AND LEARN

Copy the words on the lines provided.

1. area   _____

2. zero   _____

3. nothing   _____

4. anything   _____

5. something   _____

6. close   _____

7. love   _____

8. can't   _____

9. cannot   _____

10. let's   _____

11. important   _____

12. begin   _____

SPELLING TEST 1: SIGHT WORDS

*Time to do some wordcrafting! Have a parent or friend read the words from **page 115** to you and see how many you can spell correctly.*

Date:

_____

Number correct:

_____

1. _____

2. _____

3. _____

4. _____

5. _____

6. _____

7. _____

8. _____

9. _____

10. _____

11. _____

12. _____

SIGHT WORD REVIEW: COPY AND LEARN

Copy the words on the lines provided.

1. every _____

2. high _____

3. near _____

4. between _____

5. own _____

6. easy _____

7. always _____

8. thought _____

9. start _____

10. city _____

11. school _____

12. front _____

SPELLING TEST 2: SIGHT WORDS

*Time to do some wordcrafting! Have a parent or friend read the words from **page 117** to you and see how many you can spell correctly.*

Date:

_____

Number correct:

_____

1. _____

2. _____

3. _____

4. _____

5. _____

6. _____

7. _____

8. _____

9. _____

10. _____

11. _____

12. _____

SIGHT WORD REVIEW: COPY AND LEARN

Copy the words on the lines provided.

1. today _____

2. yesterday _____

3. together _____

4. child _____

5. children _____

6. idea _____

7. young _____

8. being _____

9. sometimes _____

10. copy _____

11. without _____

12. perfect _____

SPELLING TEST 3: SIGHT WORDS

*Time to do some wordcrafting! Have a parent or friend read the words from **page 119** to you and see how many you can spell correctly.*

Date:

_____

Number correct:

_____

1. _____

2. _____

3. _____

4. _____

5. _____

6. _____

7. _____

8. _____

9. _____

10. _____

11. _____

12. _____

SIGHT WORD REVIEW: COPY AND LEARN

Copy the words on the lines provided.

1. fly   _____

2. food   _____

3. off   _____

4. took   _____

5. talk   _____

6. list   _____

7. quiet   _____

8. visit   _____

9. almost   _____

10. buy   _____

11. once   _____

12. water   _____

SPELLING TEST 4: SIGHT WORDS

*Time to do some wordcrafting! Have a parent or friend read the words from **page 121** to you and see how many you can spell correctly.*

Date:

_____

Number correct:

_____

1. _____

2. _____

3. _____

4. _____

5. _____

6. _____

7. _____

8. _____

9. _____

10. _____

11. _____

12. _____

ANSWERS

**PAGE 68,
WORD FILL-IN**

1. next (short)
2. Keep (long)
3. safe (long)
4. stand (short)
5. best (short)

**PAGE 69,
STEVE'S WORD SCRAMBLE**

1. dress (short)
2. save (long)
3. plant (short)
4. reach (long)
5. grade (long)

**PAGE 70,
ORDER CHALLENGE**

1. between
2. easy
3. every
4. high
5. near
6. own

**PAGE 71,
FIND AND FIX**

1. easy
2. every
3. near
4. own
5. between
6. high

**PAGE 73,
WITHER'S WORD SEARCH**

```
S T V D H R B O Z P Y Z
A Z S I R E E D W T T Q
F J G E T E G A R N Z N
E H A W B R S R C J N N
T S E L Y S B S A H R D
Y E D R L T V W N D X L
N T E D Y A V D P T E V
P V X N T N X L N E A R
E E T E K D A Y V T L J
Z T E M N N X A L Y Q J
B B X K T M S L D R L Z
```

**PAGE 74,
WORD FILL-IN**

1. cute (long)
2. slip (short)
3. stop (short)
4. groan (long)
5. ride (long)

**PAGE 75,
STEVE'S WORD SCRAMBLE**

1. rock (short)
2. sing (short)
3. hope (long)
4. jump (short)
5. dive (long)

**PAGE 78,
RHYME BLOCKS**

Rhyming words may vary. Some answers include:

1. bump, dump, hump, lump
2. dock, jock, knock, lock, mock, sock
3. art, cart, dart, fart, heart, tart
4. bought, caught, fought, ought, sought, taught
5. cool, drool, fool, ghoul, rule, tool
6. dried, fried, guide, side, tied, tried, wide

PAGE 79,
WITHER'S WORD SEARCH

```
P R I D E E T G S R
M L W V A H P T L V
U C I G O L A O R Z
J D U U R R W N H S
G L G T T O Y A L R
F H O S E T A I Y S
T R I O I R P N T S
V N O C H O M O K R
G X T N M C P Q B T
D Q Z R T K S P P G
```

PAGE 80,
END BLENDS

1. enou<u>gh</u>
2. bea<u>ch</u>
3. wa<u>tch</u>
4. bo<u>th</u>
5. cra<u>sh</u>

PAGE 82,
GROWING WORDS

1. area
2. zero
3. close
4. nothing
5. anything
6. something

PAGE 83,
FIND AND FIX

1. Nothing
2. something
3. area
4. anything
5. close
6. zero

PAGE 85,
WITHER'S WORD SEARCH

```
Z K N K G D Q D M X B L P
E K T A E N H G U O N E H
R Y D S N T I B L D D C R
O H O G O Y Y H G T A Q J
Y L P B R Q T N T E M G Y
C A Y A W A I H B O M L B
M U H Y R H P X I A N L M
D G Z S T G L H T N P Z L
A H P E A Y O C B H G X D
G E M U R R H T C T Y T B
X O R Q S N C T O D P N B
S B P A M H A N D H R Y Q
K B G L D W X B D V P K L
```

PAGE 86,
SOFT SOUNDS

1. c
2. g
3. c
4. g
5. c

PAGE 89,
STEVE'S WORD SCRAMBLE

1. begin (2)
2. can't (1)
3. important (3)
4. love (1)
5. cannot (2)

PAGE 91, WITHER'S WORD SEARCH

```
Y N M B P Y L W W E Y Y N X
L L D D R R J J E R C E T T
E T D J M Y Y B K N C N B B
T T L I C N E P A I E A N
' L Y O I Z D Y P J C G I D
S B P D N M T S N I P G N K
C P D M E N P Y L N E G E E
P A B C R B A O Z B I G V M
G E N T L E P C R R A O D K
Q E P ' D N Y K A T L N T P
F M R D T T Y F S M A Y T B
M T I V Y L F D N M T N R M
J Y C X B E N R N B L Q T Q
V N E K W P R N B N T T P Q
```

PAGE 92, GLIDING VOWELS

1. oi
2. oy
3. ou
4. ow
5. ou

PAGE 94, ORDER CHALLENGE

1. child
2. children
3. idea
4. today
5. together
6. yesterday

PAGE 96, FIND AND FIX

1. noise
2. together
3. mouth
4. today
5. brown
6. idea

PAGE 97, WITHER'S WORD SEARCH

```
M J M M L N A L K D N Z N L K
R J T L N J B E M J B M Z J D
N Y R N Z G R Y D C H I L D J
R E H T E G O T A I J Y B L T
N F R D I H C J D A J R M G
M X B N N J Y T B D O N L Z E
B O K L P U L D R Z G T N C M
R D U L N N O E P R X T I O R
O N T N Q W T R O Y U O U V Y
W T O R T S O U A O H T L M Y
N L Y I E A N R H C H N Y V T
M W J Y S D I S C G Y L L X K
Q L Z D N E Y N D Y T Q K R V
```

PAGE 98, WHICH IS IT?

1. here
2. way
3. bored
4. bear
5. flower

PAGE 99, RHYME BLOCKS

Rhyming words may vary. Some answers include:

1. dear, deer, fear, gear, near, peer, pier, rear
2. bay, day, hay, lay, may, okay, pay, say
3. cored, cord, ford, lord, sword, ward, warred
4. air, care, dare, fair, fare, hair, hare, mare, rare, wear
5. hour, power, sour, tower

125

PAGE 100,
GROWING WORDS

1. copy
2. being
3. young
4. perfect
5. without
6. sometimes

PAGE 101,
STEVE'S WORD SCRAMBLE

1. sometimes (2)
2. perfect (2)
3. without (2)
4. being (2)
5. young (1)

PAGE 103,
WITHER'S WORD SEARCH

PAGE 104,
SEEING DOUBLE

1. pp
2. nn
3. rr
4. pp
5. ll

PAGE 105,
FIND AND FIX

1. bottle
2. correct
3. lesson
4. common
5. collect

PAGE 108,
ORDER CHALLENGE

1. fly
2. food
3. list
4. off
5. talk
6. took

PAGE 109,
WITHER'S WORD SEARCH

PAGE 110,
BUILDING COMPOUNDS

1. sun
2. book
3. foot
4. bow
5. water

PAGE 112, GROWING WORDS

1. buy
2. once
3. quiet
4. visit
5. water
6. almost

PAGE 113, FIND AND FIX

1. almost
2. visit
3. quiet
4. Once
5. water
6. buy

PAGE 114, WITHER'S WORD SEARCH

```
F L E H S K O O B O N C E
W V N S R O O D T U O T G
M A M O D T T T E P E G R
F B T O T S I V Y S W M N
W O D E O E E S N T S M X
O D O M R R B U I U L Y W
B K L T Y F S O N V T M B
N A J O B T A S O W Z M T
I R N R E A H L A K Z R M
A E B I Y I L T L L D B G
R T U U N L E L Q R C D J
N Q L E Y R N R W L B R T
```

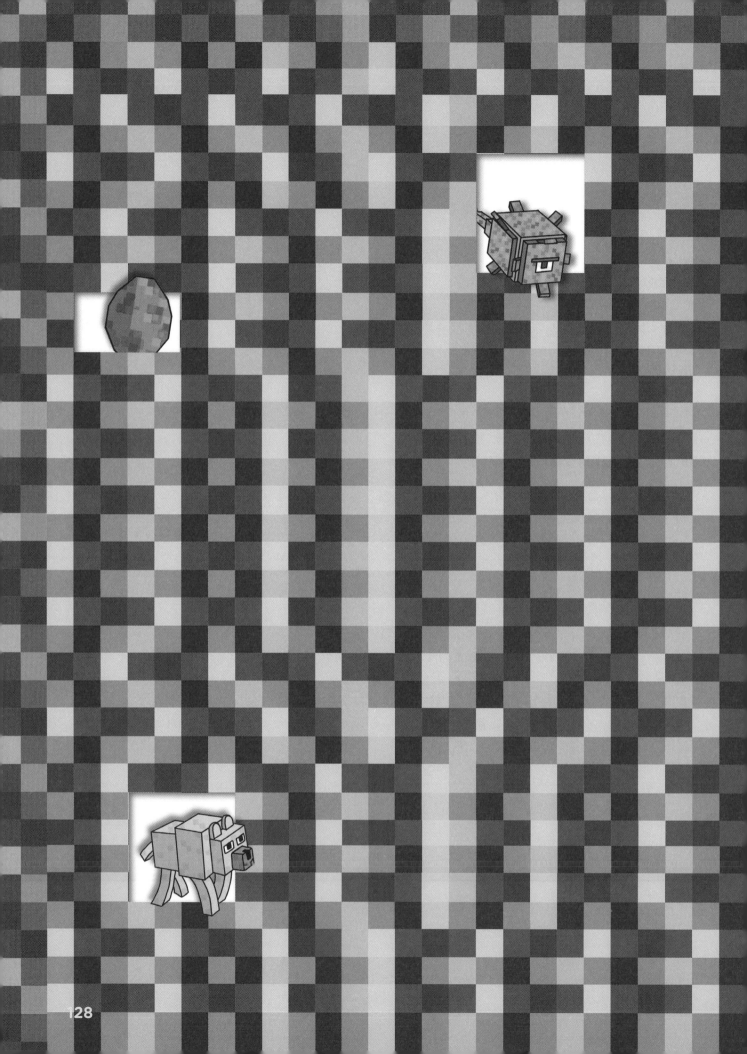

CHAPTER THREE

WRITING WITH STEVE AND ALEX

WRITE WHAT YOU KNOW

Look at the characters below. Finish the sentence about each Minecrafting character or mob using what you see or know. The first one is done for you.

1.  Steve is wearing  blue pants .

2.  Alex likes _____ .

3.  The Enderman is _____ .

4  A diamond sword is _____ .

5.  A chest is good for _____ .

6.  The Ender dragon can ....

7. The Wither has ....

8. The Guardian has ....

9. A zombie will ....

10. A skeleton is ....

CREEPER'S GUIDE TO COLLECTIVE NOUNS

Collective nouns *are words used to describe groups of items.*
For example, a group of birds is also called a **flock** *of birds.*

Highlight or circle the words below that are collective nouns:

pack	team	army	mushroom
zombie	herd	creeper	stack

Choose three collective nouns above and use them to write
sentences about Minecrafting.

1. _____

_____

_____

2. _____

_____

_____

3. _____

_____

_____

Match the collective noun to the group it best describes.

1. bouquet

2. family

3. flock

4. school

5. forest

6. pile

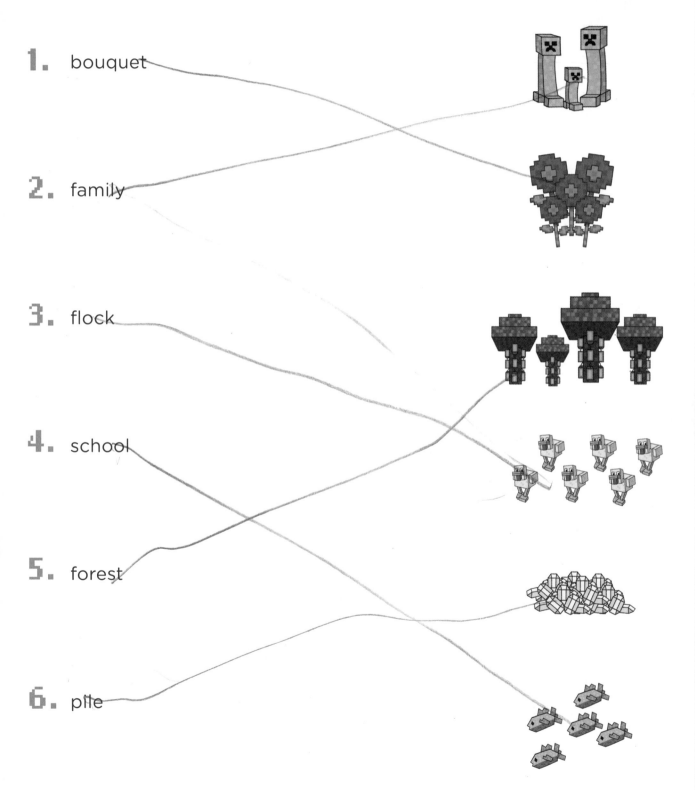

SILLY FILL-IN

Fill in the word blanks below. Read the story at right and add your words as you go. Did it make you laugh?

ADJECTIVE
a describing word,
like *scary*

NOUN
a person, place or
thing, like *creeper*

VERB
an action word,
like *run*

1. _____
   ADJECTIVE

2. _____
   ADJECTIVE

3. _____
   NOUN

4. _____
   ANIMAL

5. _____
   PLACE IN MINECRAFT

6. _____
   NUMBER

7. _____
   VERB

8. _____
   ADJECTIVE

9. _____
   SAME ANIMAL AS #4

10. _____
    PLACE IN MINECRAFT

11. _____
    ADJECTIVE

A WITCHY DAY

The witch was having a/an ___Smelly___ day, so she
ADJECTIVE

decided to make a/an ___void___ potion using
ADJECTIVE

___bedrock___ as the main ingredient. She thought it would
NOUN

be funny to throw the potion at a/an ___cow___ ,
ANIMAL

who was in the ___Ice___ . It took ___3___
PLACE IN MINECRAFT   NUMBER

minutes to ___run___ there. When she opened her
VERB

bag, though, she realized the potion was ___Skuck___ !
ADJECTIVE

The ___cow___ ran off. She gave up and decided
SAME ANIMAL

to go to ___the end___ instead, which was much more
PLACE IN MINECRAFT

___Happy___ .
ADJECTIVE

SENTENCES

A **sentence** is a group of words that tells a complete thought. All sentences begin with a **capital letter**. A statement ends with a **period**. A sentence includes a **noun**, a **verb**, and sometimes an **adjective**.

ADJECTIVE
a describing word, like *scary*

NOUN
a person, place or thing, like *creeper*

VERB
an action word, like *run*

Read the sentences on the opposite page and follow the instructions below.

✦ Draw a triangle around the **capital letter** that begins the sentence.

✦ Circle the **noun** (there may be more than one).

✦ Underline the **verb**.

✦ Draw a rectangle around the **adjective**.

✦ Draw a square around the **period** that ends the sentence.

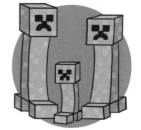

1. 　The hungry horse eats a carrot.

2. 　The villager trades with a player.

3. 　Alex rides a pig.

4. 　The nervous creeper explodes.

5. 　The skeleton shoots an arrow.

137

IN THE JUNGLE

Pretend you spawn (start in the game) in the jungle biome.
Describe how you would survive. Use details.

If I spawned in the jungle, I would

_____

_____

_____

_____

_____

_____

_____

If I needed food I would.....

_____

_____

_____

_____

Finally, I would stay safe by...

_____

_____

_____

_____

_____

_____

PLURAL NOUNS

Rewrite the sentences. Change the noun in parentheses into a plural noun and write it on the line. The first one is done for you.

~~feet~~	~~leaves~~	~~shelves~~
~~Endermen~~	~~children~~	~~wolves~~

1. The creeper has block-shaped (foot) __feet__ .

2. Steve likes to tame (wolf) __wolves__ and keep them as pets.

3. There are lots of (Enderman) __Endermen__ on the other side of this portal.

4. Many (child) __children__ play Minecraft.

5. Lily pads are (leaf) __leaves__ that float.

6. There are plenty of books on these (shelf) __shelves__ .

139

DESCRIBING IN DETAIL

Use the word box to help you write 5 sentences about the picture below. Remember to use capital letters at the beginning of each sentence and a period at the end.

poster   laptop   sticker   sword   mug

pig   creeper   kids   shelves

1.

2.

3.

4.

5.

COMPARE AND CONTRAST

Fill in the Venn Diagram with similarities and differences between your bedroom and the one shown in the picture on the previous page.

BEDROOM
IN PICTURE

MY
BEDROOM

BOTH

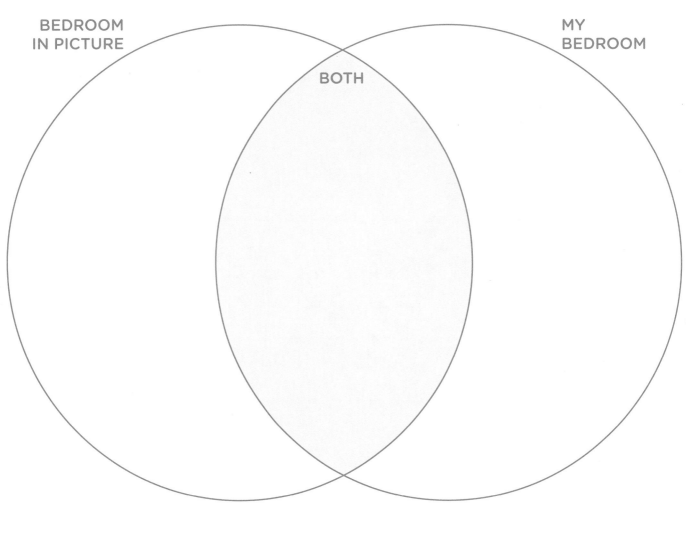

Write one complete sentence describing a difference.

_____

_____

_____

_____

Write one complete sentence describing a similarity.

_____

_____

_____

IRREGULAR PAST TENSE VERBS

Fill in the blanks with these irregular past tense verbs.

| sat | ~~ran~~ | ~~fought~~ | ~~took~~ | ~~gave~~ |

1. The iron golem _gave_ a flower to the villager.

2. Steve _fought_ the wither with all his strength.

3. Alex _ran_ away from an army of skeletons.

4. The chicken _sat_ on a creeper spawn egg by mistake.

5. The thief _took_ everything out of my chest.

WRITE YOUR OPINION

Which of these items is most useful when Minecrafting? Choose one and complete the paragraph below.

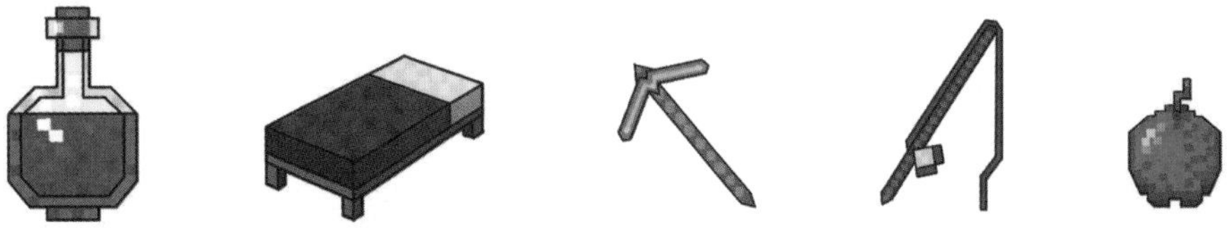

A _____ is the most useful item because

_____

_____

_____

_____ .

You can also use this item to _____

_____

_____ .

Finally, it's _____

_____

_____ .

In conclusion, _____ is the most useful item of all the

items above.

144

WRITING A NARRATIVE

The four pictures below tell a story. Use the pictures to help you tell the story of Alex and Steve trying to get a cow back to its pen. Use the back of the page if needed.

1. 2. 3. 4.

WRITING A NARRATIVE

(continued)

USING DETAILS

Match the sentence to its more detailed version.

1. The Enderman moved toward Steve.

A. The End is a dangerous world where you can battle a dragon

2. The zombie appeared.

B. Alex uses her pickaxe to mine for lapis lazuli.

3. Alex mines for lapis lazuli.

C. The zombie appeared out of nowhere in gold armor.

4. Diamond swords can destroy things.

D. The tall Enderman teleported toward Steve when Steve made eye contact.

5. The End is dangerous.

E. Diamond swords can destroy blazes, Endermen, and zombies.

ADDING DETAILS

Change the sentences below. Add details to make them more interesting or exciting.

1. I see a villager.

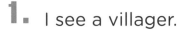

2. The wolf is hungry.

3. I am building a shelter.

4. I have resources.

5. I fight a creeper.

CONTRACTIONS

Draw a line connecting each pair of words with its contraction.

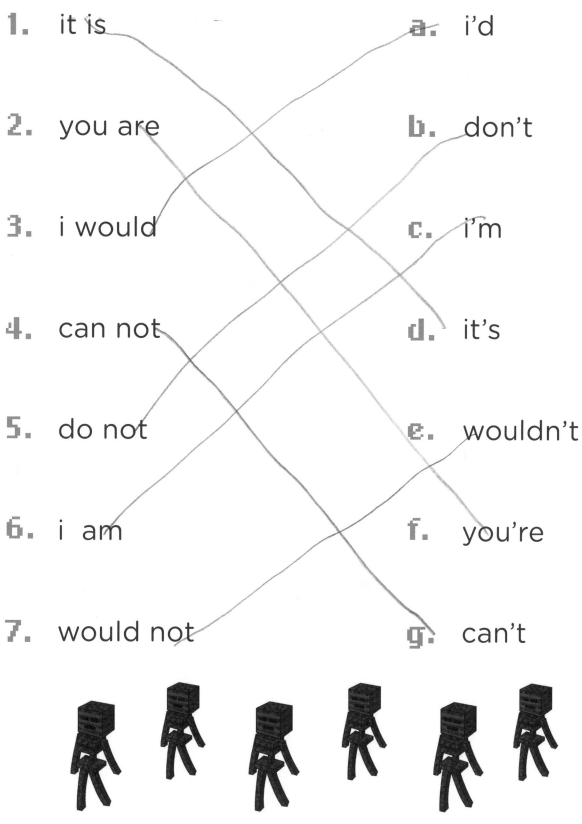

1. it is
2. you are
3. i would
4. can not
5. do not
6. i am
7. would not

a. i'd
b. don't
c. i'm
d. it's
e. wouldn't
f. you're
g. can't

CONTRACTIONS

Write the correct contraction on the space provided. Don't forget the apostrophe!

1. Most players _____ survive a Wither attack.
   CAN NOT

2. If you are building a house in Minecraft, _____ forget
   DO NOT

   to add doors to keep out hostile mobs.

3. When _____ learning to play, set the difficulty to
   YOU ARE

   Peaceful or Easy mode.

4. I _____ get too close to a creeper that's
   WOULD NOT

   about to explode.

   Write your own Minecrafting sentence below using a contraction from
   page 149.

   _____

   _____

   _____

   _____

SILLY FILL-IN

Fill in the word blanks below. Read the story on the next page and add your words as you go. Did it make you laugh?

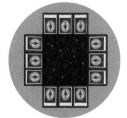

ADJECTIVE
a describing word,
like *scary*

NOUN
a person, place or
thing, like *creeper*

VERB
an action word,
like *run*

1. _____
   PLACE

2. _____
   VERB

3. _____
   VERB

4. _____
   VERB, PAST TENSE

5. _____
   VERB

6. _____
   VERB

7. _____
   PART OF THE BODY

8. _____
   ADJECTIVE

9. _____
   VERB

10. _____
    ADJECTIVE

11. _____
    NOUN

12. _____
    VERB

13. _____
    NOUN

14. _____
    VERB

15. _____
    ADJECTIVE

16. _____
    SCHOOL SUBJECT

ENDER DRAGON GOES TO THE DENTIST

One day, Steve went to __Durham__ to __Pee__
                  PLACE   **VERB**

the Ender dragon. Before he could __Poop__ his
                             VERB

diamond sword, the Ender dragon stopped him. "I can't fight you

today," he __~~has~~ Peed__ . My tooth is aching so badly, I want
           VERB, PAST TENSE

to __Poo__ ." "__Poop__ with me," said Steve,
      VERB   **VERB**

and he took the dragon by the __eye__ and led him
                    PART OF THE BODY

through the End portal to a __white__ village." This dentist
                     ADJECTIVE

villager can __Poop__ you and make you feel more
                   VERB

__boring__ ," Steve explained. The Ender dragon was
     ADJECTIVE

nervous, but he sat ~~in a~~ __steve__ in the dentist's office and let
                NOUN

him __Poo__ the sore tooth. The more nervous the dragon
      VERB

became, the more he breathed __Steve__ . Steve used a potion
                  NOUN

of heat resistance to __Poop__ the dentist, but by the time the
              VERB

appointment was over, the dentist was very __Smelly__ . When
                            ADJECTIVE

the dragon left, the dentist breathed a heavy sigh of relief and said, "If

only I had listened to my mother and studied __Math__ ."
                                       SCHOOL SUBJECT

NOUNS IN THE NETHER

Use the **nouns** in the box to complete the sentences about the Nether. Remember, a noun is a person, a place, or a thing.

mushrooms	portal	obsidian	fire	zombie pigman

1. _____ grow all over the ground in the Nether.

2. The Nether is filled with _____ , lava, and dangerous mobs.

3. A _____ is the only way to get to the Nether.

4. You need _____ to build a portal.

5. You can battle a blaze, a ghast, or a _____ _____ in the Nether.

VERBS WITH VILLAGERS

*Use **the verbs** in the box to complete the sentences about villagers. Remember, verbs are action words, like "jump," "make," and "eat."*

plant	trade	run	strikes	become

1. Villagers will _____ you for emeralds.

2. Villagers will _____ away if a zombie attacks.

3. If a zombie attacks a villager, the villager could _____ a zombie villager.

4. A farming villager will _____ and tend crops.

5. If lightning _____ a villager, it turns into a witch.

MINING FOR ADJECTIVES

Use the **adjectives** in the box to complete the sentences about Minecraft. Remember, **adjectives** are describing words, like "funny" and "red."

purple	icy	hostile	poisonous	wooden

1. Polar bears live in _____ biomes.

2. Pufferfish are _____ in the game of Minecraft.

3. A _____ shield will protect you in battle.

4. The shulker hides in its _____ shell.

5. A slime is a _____ mob that hops around.

WRITING IN PAST TENSE

*Use the **past tense** to finish the sentence about how you used to play Minecraft when you were a noob (someone who is new to gaming).*

When I was a noob, I...

1.

2.

3.

4.

UNDERWATER FUN

Minecraft is going aquatic! Study the picture for a minute or two. When you think you have memorized the details, try to answer the questions on the back of the page without looking!

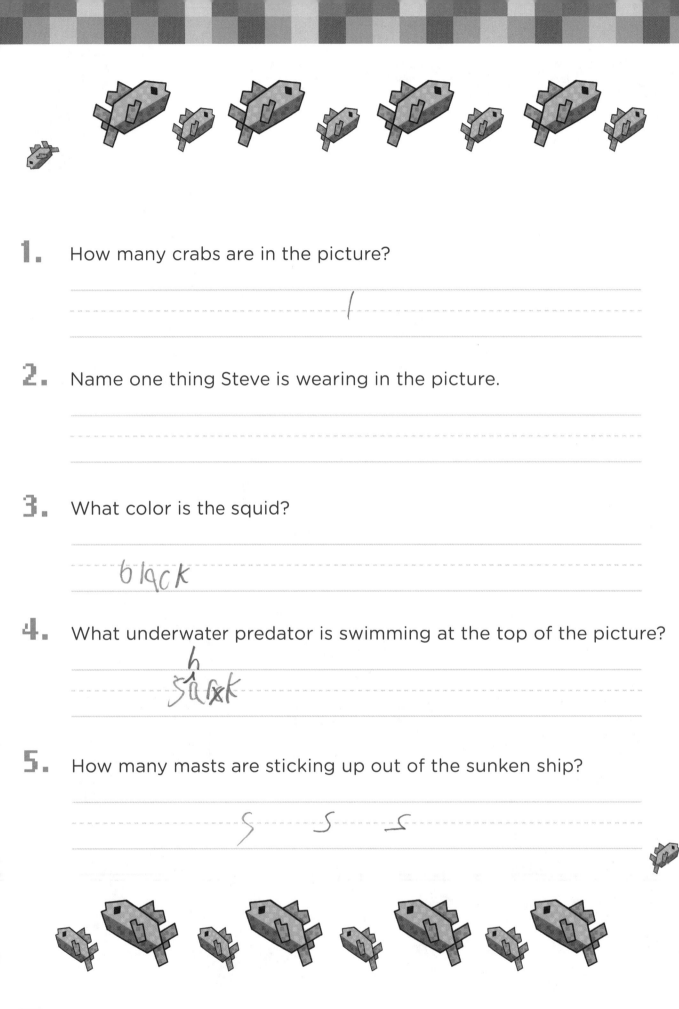

1. How many crabs are in the picture?

/

2. Name one thing Steve is wearing in the picture.

3. What color is the squid?

black

4. What underwater predator is swimming at the top of the picture?

shark

5. How many masts are sticking up out of the sunken ship?

5 5 5

PUNCTUATE IT!

Every sentence should have a capital letter in the beginning and punctuation (like a period) at the end. These sentences are missing both. Write them correctly on the line below.

1. the baby zombie rides a chicken

2. you can tame an ocelot

3. a golden apple can heal you

4. watch out for the zombie pigman

5. don't eat a puffer fish

MIX IT UP!

Put the words in these mixed-up sentences in the correct order. Add a capital letter in the beginning of the sentence and a punctuation mark at the end.

1. amazing Steve an is builder

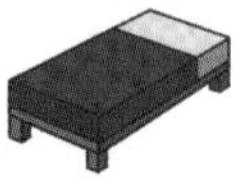

2. builds Steve bed a

3. is the attacking skeleton

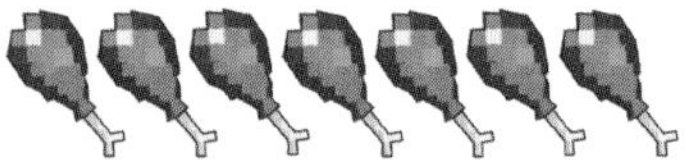

4. bar is hunger my low

5. night come out at zombies

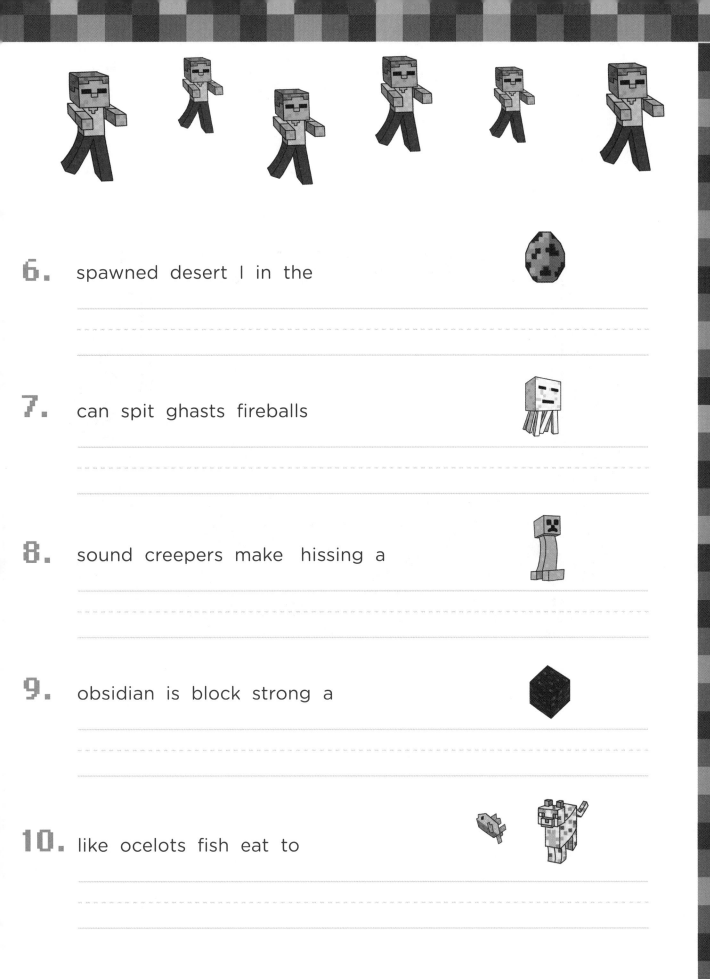

6. spawned desert I in the

_____

_____

_____

7. can spit ghasts fireballs

_____

_____

_____

8. sound creepers make hissing a

_____

_____

_____

9. obsidian is block strong a

_____

_____

_____

10. like ocelots fish eat to

_____

_____

_____

WRITING A NARRATIVE

Someone hid a very valuable object or a secret room behind this Minecraft painting. Write a story where you walk through this mysterious painting. Describe what you discover on the other side and what happens next.

Use the sentence starters below for help:

When I walked through the painting, I saw...   Next, I...

Suddenly, I...   Then I...

I couldn't believe...   Finally, I...

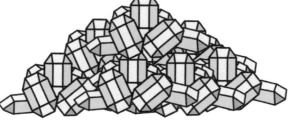

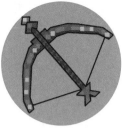

SO MUCH TO DO

Fill in Alex's weekly planner. Use the pictures to help you guess what she wants to do each day. Use a verb (action word) in every entry. Be creative!

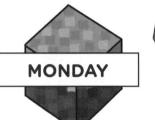

MONDAY

 brew some potion

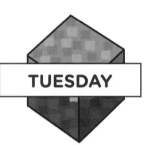

TUESDAY

WEDNESDAY

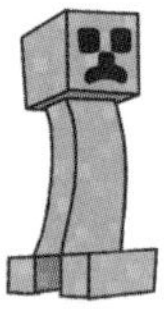

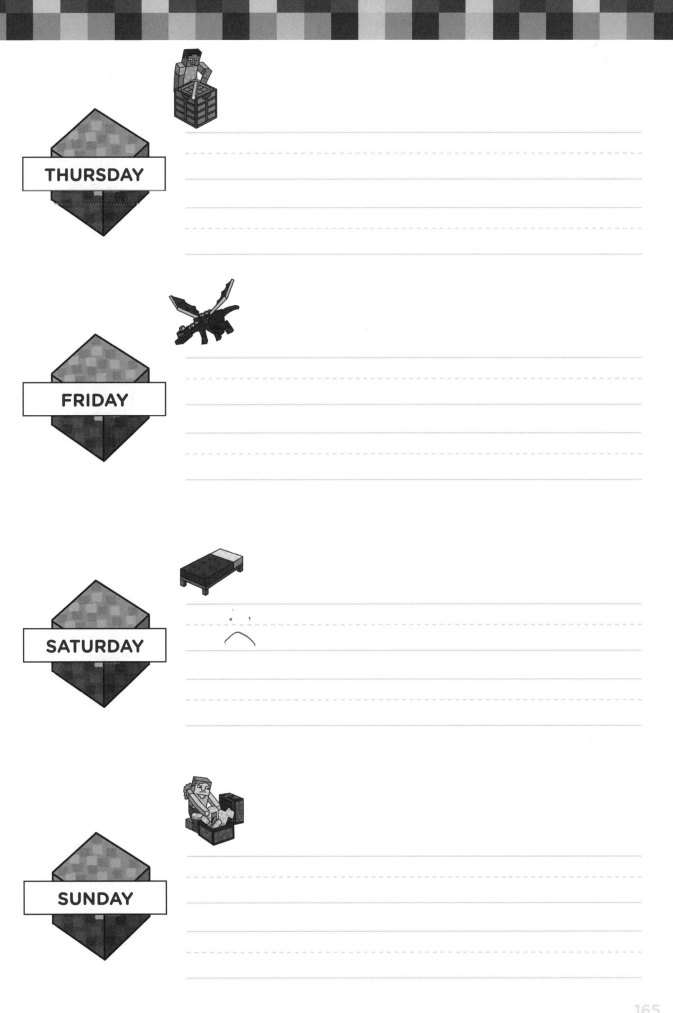

THURSDAY

FRIDAY

SATURDAY

SUNDAY

SENTENCE GRIEFER

A griefer (a gamer who likes to trick other gamers) wrote these false sentences about Minecrafting. Use the contractions in the word box to make them true. The first one has been done for you. Hint: One contraction is used twice.

don't	aren't	can't	isn't

1. Witches **do** attack villagers.

Witches don't attack villagers

2. Skeletons **are** peaceful mobs.

_____

_____

3. Zombies **are** safe in the sunlight.

_____

_____

4. Creepers **can** open doors.

_____

_____

5. An enderman **is** an undead mob.

_____

_____

WRITING A TO-DO LIST

Make a Minecrafting TO DO List that includes all the things you want to experience or try in Minecraft.

Things I Want to Do/Learn in Minecraft:

-
-
-
-
-
-
-
-

REFLEXIVE PRONOUNS

Rewrite the words in the word box under the correct category: reflexive pronouns or nouns. Hint: Reflexive pronouns are like mirrors: They reflect back to the subject.

~~itself~~	creeper	himself	skeleton	Wither
themselves	ourselves	villager	myself	

REFLEXIVE PRONOUNS

1. itself
2.
3.
4.
5.

NOUNS

1.
2.
3.
4.

HOW TO BUILD A GOLEM

A snow golem is helpful for defending you from hostile mobs. Read the directions for building a Snow Golem. Use the words at the beginning of the sentences to number them in the correct order.

_____ Finally, enjoy watching your snow golem shoot snowballs at your enemies!

_____ Second, stack the two snow blocks on top of each other.

_____ First, make sure you have two snow blocks and a pumpkin in your inventory.

_____ After you stack the snow blocks, place the pumpkin on top of them.

WRITE WHAT YOU KNOW

Look at the Minecrafting pictures below. Finish the sentence about each picture using what you see and know.

1. Steve is crafting a

2.  The spider has

3.  The squid can

4.  A bow-and-arrow can

5.  Steve holds a

6. The boat is made of _____ .

7. This chest is _____ .

8. Steve has a _____ .

9. Steve feels _____ .

10. The pig is wearing a _____ .

CREEPER'S COLLECTIVE NOUNS

*Match the **collective noun** to the group it best describes.*

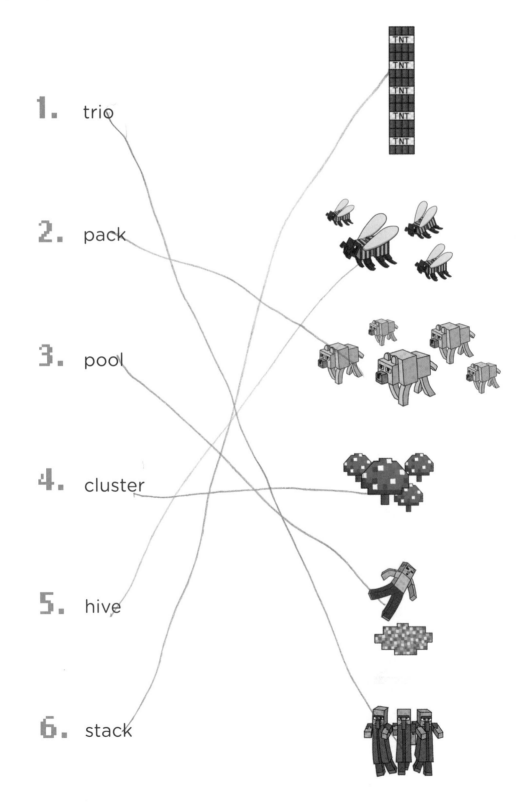

1. trio

2. pack

3. pool

4. cluster

5. hive

6. stack

SILLY FILL-IN

Fill in the word blanks below. Read the story on the next page and add your words as you go. Did it make you laugh?

ADJECTIVE
a describing word, like *scary*

NOUN
a person, place or thing, like *creeper*

VERB
an action word, like *run*

ADVERB
a word that describes how you do something, like *slowly*

1. _____
   NOUN

2. _____
   PLURAL NOUN

3. _____
   VERB

4. _____
   PLURAL NOUN

5. _____
   NOUN

6. _____
   PLURAL NOUN

7. _____
   ADVERB

8. _____
   PLURAL NOUN

9. _____
   PLURAL NOUN

10. _____
    ANIMAL

11. _____
    ADJECTIVE

12. _____
    NOUN

13. _____
    ADJECTIVE

14. _____
    VERB

15. _____
    ADJECTIVE

A TRIP TO THE NETHER

Before you enter the Nether, you should know that it's full of

flowing _____ and pools of _____. The
　　　　　　　NOUN　　　　　　　　　　　　　　　PLURAL NOUN

only reason players dare to _____ here is because it's
　　　　　　　　　　　　　　　　VERB

full of useful _____ like nether _____ and
　　　　　　　　PLURAL NOUN　　　　　　　　　　　　NOUN

blaze _____. Get those items as _____
　　　　PLURAL NOUN　　　　　　　　　　　　　　ADVERB

as you can before hostile _____ start to attack. If a
　　　　　　　　　　　　　　PLURAL NOUN

ghast starts spitting _____ at you, you might be in big
　　　　　　　　　　　　PLURAL NOUN

trouble. Watch out for zombie _____ men, too. They are
　　　　　　　　　　　　　　　　ANIMAL

_____ and carry a wooden _____. If you
　　ADJECTIVE　　　　　　　　　　　　　　　　NOUN

become surrounded by _____ mobs in the Nether, the
　　　　　　　　　　　　ADJECTIVE

best thing to do is _____ to the portal and get back to the
　　　　　　　　　　VERB

Overworld before it's too _____.
　　　　　　　　　　　　ADJECTIVE

IN THE EXTREME HILLS BIOME

Pretend you spawn (start in the game) in the Extreme Hills Biome. Describe how you would survive. Use details.

If I spawned in the Extreme Hills Biome, I would...

_____

_____

_____

_____

_____

_____

_____

If I needed food I would...

_____

_____

_____

_____

Finally, I would stay safe by...

_____

_____

_____

_____

_____

SENTENCES

*A **sentence** is a group of words that tells a complete thought. All sentences begin with a **capital letter**. A statement ends with a **period**. A sentence includes a **noun**, a **verb**, and sometimes an **adjective**.*

| **ADJECTIVE** a describing word, like *scary* | **NOUN** a person, place or thing, like *creeper* | **VERB** an action word, like *run* |

1. Draw a triangle around the **capital letter** that begins the sentence.

2. Circle the **noun** (there may be more than one).

3. Underline the **verb**.

4. Draw a rectangle around the **adjective**.

5. Draw a square around the **period** that ends the sentence.

1.  This stew restores my hunger.

2.  The skeleton shot me with an arrow.

3.  That witch threw a splash potion.

4.  An oven cooks raw meat.

5. 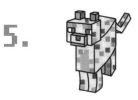 An ocelot eats fish.

PLURAL NOUNS

Rewrite the sentences. Change the noun in parentheses to a plural noun and write it on the line. The first one is done for you.

teeth	lives	puppies
witches	people	

1. The (witch) __witches__ live in the swamp biome.

2. Multi-player mode lets you play with other (person) _____.

3. Zombies prefer to live their (life) _____ in the dark.

4. Tame (puppy) _____ will follow their owner around.

5. Creepers do not have any (tooth) _____.

COMPARE AND CONTRAST

Compare these two hostile mobs. How are they the same?
Write things that are the same about them in the center of
the diagram. Which one is scarier? Bigger? Describe their
differences on the sides.

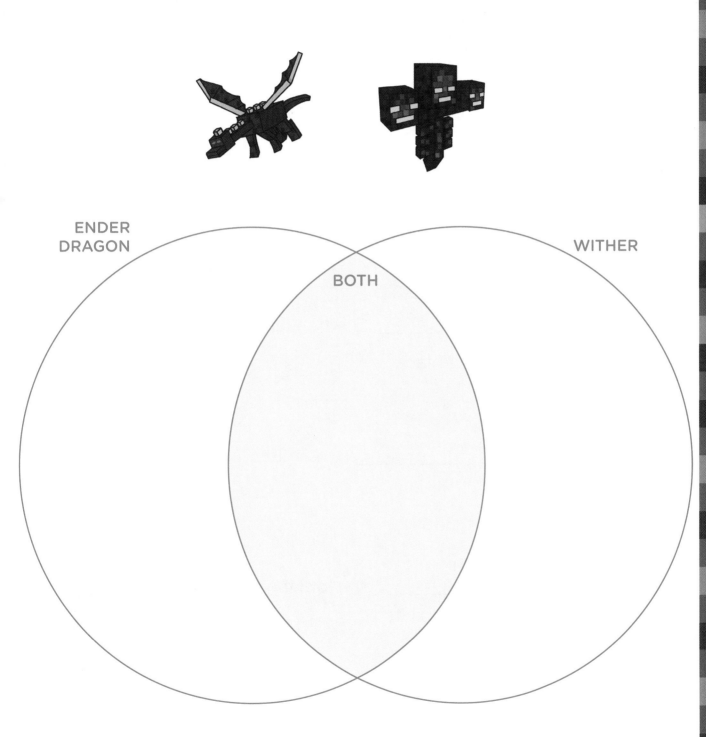

ENDER
DRAGON

BOTH

WITHER

IRREGULAR PAST TENSE VERBS

Fill in the blanks with these irregular past tense verbs.

~~made~~	~~brought~~	~~flew~~	~~saw~~	grew

1. Alex __brought__ her golden sword with her to the End.

2. Steve's flower __grew__ when he placed bone meal on a grass black.

3. The Ender dragon __flew__ to an End crystal to regain health.

4. The Enderman __saw__ me looking at it and teleported over.

5. Steve __made__ a fishing rod from three sticks and two pieces of string .

REMEMBERING DETAILS

This gamer's bedroom is very messy! Study the picture for a minute or two. When you think you have memorized the details, try to answer the questions on the back of the page without looking!

REMEMBERING DETAILS
(continued from previous page)
Answer the questions in the space provided.

1. Name one toy on the floor of the bedroom.

ball

2. What object can be seen out the bedroom window?

Tree

3. What color is the lamp?

White

4. What is on top of the bookshelf?

Plant

5. What animal shape is hidden in several places?

cat

WRITE YOUR OPINION

Which of these mobs would be most useful to bring to school? Who could you play with at recess? Which one could carry your backpack? Who could get you to and from school the fastest? Choose one and complete the paragraph below.

iron golem   creeper   zombie   wither   snow golem

The most useful mob to take to school is a

because

A job this mob could do at my school is

In conclusion, a

is the most useful mob to bring to school.

CERTIFICATE OF ACHIEVEMENT
CONGRATULATIONS

This certifies that

TYler
_____

became a

MINECRAFT WRITING BOSS

on ___10/ 9/ 2)___ .
(date)

Tyler
_____
Signature

ANSWERS

PAGES 130-131
Write What You Know

Answers may vary, but might include the details below:

2. Alex likes animals.
3. The Enderman is tall.
4. A diamond sword is strong.
5. A chest is good for storing things.
6. The Ender dragon can fly.
7. The Wither has three heads.
8. The Guardian has fins.
9. A zombie will attack.
10. A skeleton is made of bones.

PAGES 132-133
Creeper's Guide to Collective Nouns

(pack)　(team)　(army)　mushroom

zombie　(herd)　creeper　(stack)

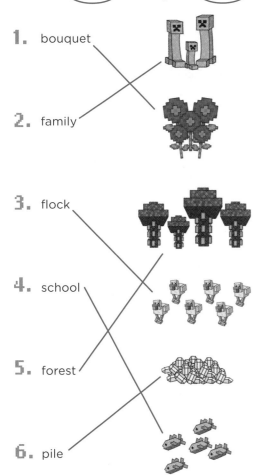

1. bouquet
2. family
3. flock
4. school
5. forest
6. pile

PAGES 134-135
Silly Fill-In
Answers will vary.

PAGES 136-137
Sentences

1. The hungry horse eats a carrot.
2. The villager trades with a player.
3. Alex rides a pig.
4. The nervous creeper explodes.
5. The skeleton shoots an arrow.

PAGE 138
In the Jungle
Answers will vary.

PAGE 139
Plural Nouns

1. feet
2. wolves
3. Endermen
4. children
5. leaves
6. shelves

PAGES 140-141
Describing in Detail
Answers will vary.

PAGE 142
Compare and Contrast
Answers will vary.

PAGE 143
Irregular Past Tense Verbs
1. gave
2. fought
3. ran
4. sat
5. took

PAGE 144
Write Your Opinion
Answers will vary.

PAGE 145–146
Writing a Narrative
Answers will vary.

PAGE 147
Using Details
1. D
2. C
3. B
4. E
5. A

PAGE 148
Adding Details
Answer will vary, but might include the details below:
1. I see a villager with his arms crossed in a white coat.
2. The white wolf is very hungry because it hasn't eaten in days.
3. I am building a house made of cobblestone and wood.
4. I have helpful resources like food and tools.
5. I fight a green creeper who is about to explode.

PAGE 149
Contractions
1. d
2. f
3. a
4. g
5. b
6. c
7. e

PAGE 150
Contractions
1. Most players **can't** survive a Wither attack.
2. If you are building a house in Minecraft, **don't** forget to add doors to keep out hostile mobs.
3. When **you're** learning to play, set the difficulty to Peaceful or Easy mode.
4. I **wouldn't** get too close to a creeper that's about to explode.

PAGES 151–152
Silly Fill-in
Answers will vary.

PAGE 153
Nouns in the Nether
1. mushrooms
2. fire
3. portal
4. obsidian
5. zombie pigman

PAGE 154
Verbs with Villagers
1. trade
2. run
3. become
4. plant
5. strikes

PAGE 155
Mining for Adjectives
1. icy
2. poisonous
3. wooden
4. purple
5. hostile

PAGE 156
Writing in Past Tense
Answers will vary.

PAGE 157–158
Underwater Fun
1. There is one crab.
2. Steve is wearing goggles. Other answers may include: scuba mask, flippers, and a wetsuit.
3. The squid is black.
4. A shark is swimming at the top of the picture.
5. The sunken ship has two masts.

PAGE 159
Punctuate It!
1. The baby zombie rides a chicken.
2. You can tame an ocelot.
3. A golden apple can heal you.
4. Watch out for the zombie pigman!
5. Don't eat a puffer fish.

PAGE 160–161
Mix it Up
1. Steve is an amazing builder.
2. Steve builds a bed.
3. The skeleton is attacking.
4. My hunger bar is low.
5. Zombies come out at night.
6. I spawned in the desert.
7. Ghasts can spit fireballs.
8. Creepers make hissing sounds.
9. Obsidian is a strong block.
10. Ocelots like to eat fish.

PAGE 162–163
Writing a Narrative
Answers will vary.

PAGE 164–165
So Much to Do
Answers will vary, but may include the following:
Tuesday: go fishing
Wednesday: battle a creeper
Thursday: craft a new weapon
Friday: fight the Ender dragon
Saturday: build a bed
Sunday: put valuable items in a chest

PAGE 166
Sentence Griefer
2. Skeletons aren't peaceful mobs.
3. Zombies aren't safe in the sunlight.
4. Creepers can't open doors.
5. An enderman isn't an undead mob.

PAGE 167
Writing a To-Do List
Answers will vary.

PAGE 168
Reflexive Pronouns
Reflexive Pronouns
itself
himself
themselves
ourselves
myself

Nouns
creeper
skeleton
Wither
villager

PAGE 169
How to Build a Golem

__4__ Finally, enjoy watching your snow golem shoot snowballs at your enemies!

__2__ Second, stack the two snow blocks on top of each other.

__1__ First, make sure you have two snow blocks and a pumpkin in your inventory.

__3__ After you stack the snow blocks, place the pumpkin on top of them.

PAGE 170-171
Write What You Know

Answers will vary but may include the following:

1. Steve is crafting a diamond sword.
2. The spider has eight legs.
3. The squid can swim.
4. A bow-and-arrow can be useful.
5. Steve holds a watering can.
6. The boat is made of wood.
7. This chest is open (or empty).
8. Stve has a pencil.
9. Steve feels surprised.
10. The pig is wearing a saddle.

PAGE 172
Creeper's Collective Nouns

1. f
2. c
3. e
4. d
5. b
6. a

PAGE 173
Silly Fill-In
Answers will vary.

PAGE 175
In the Extreme Hills Biome
Answers will vary.

PAGE 176-177
Sentences

1. This (stew) restores my (hunger).
2. The (skeleton) shot me with an (arrow).
3. That (witch) threw a splash (potion).
4. An (oven) cooks raw (meat).
5. An (ocelot) eats (fish).

PAGE 178
Plural Nouns

2. people
3. lives
4. puppies
5. teeth

PAGE 179
Compare and Contrast

Answers will vary but may include the following:

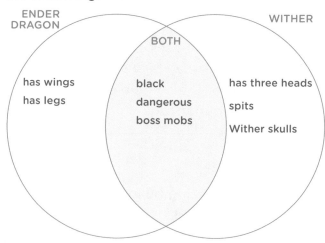

ENDER DRAGON
- has wings
- has legs

BOTH
- black
- dangerous
- boss mobs

WITHER
- has three heads
- spits
- Wither skulls

PAGE 180
Irregular Past Tense Verbs

1. brought
2. grew
3. flew
4. saw
5. made

PAGE 181-182
Remembering Details

1. There is a soccer ball (as well as a yo-yo, doll, truck, and board game).
2. A tree can be seen through the window.
3. The lamp is purple.
4. There is a plant on top of the bookshelf.
5. A pig shape is hidden in several places.

PAGE 183
Write Your Opinion

Answers will vary.

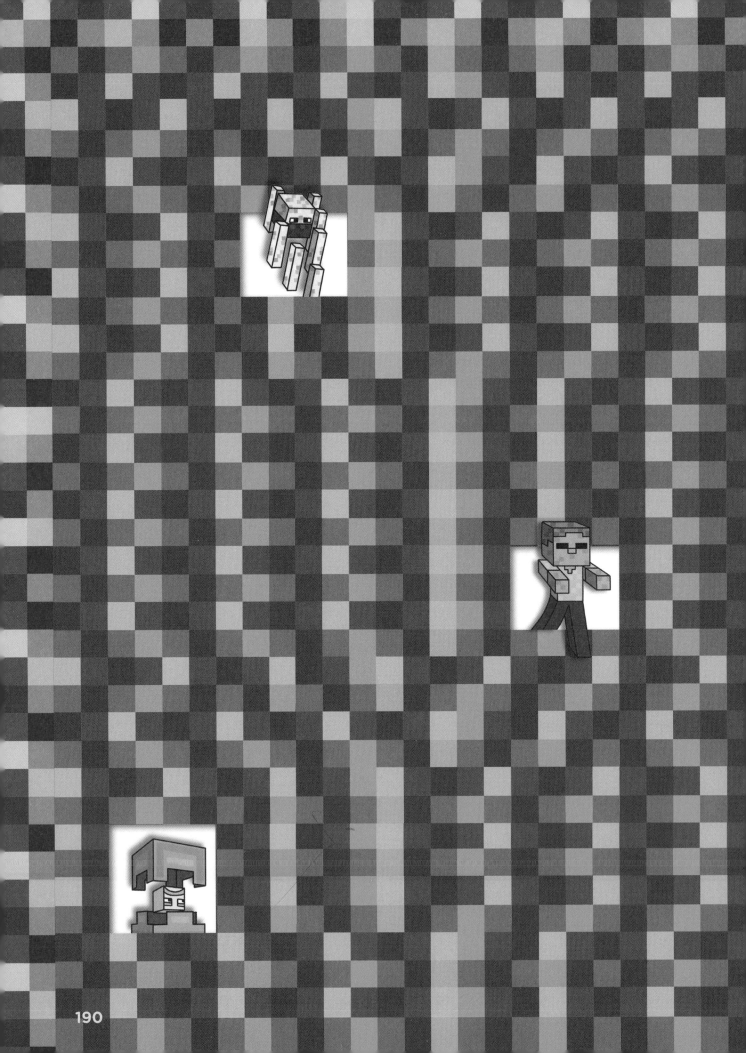

CHAPTER FOUR

S.T.E.M. CHALLENGES FOR MINECRAFTERS

THE PHYSICS OF FORCE

To smash a block, a Minecrafter must apply a *force* to the block. You apply a force to the pedals when you ride a bike. You apply a force to the ground when you walk. You apply a force to a ball when you throw or kick it.

DRAW AN ARROW SHOWING THE DIRECTION THAT STEVE WILL SWING THE PICKAXE AND APPLY FORCE TO THIS BLOCK.

Now draw your own diagram showing an example of forces at work in the game of Minecraft. Use arrows to show the direction of the forces.

2D + 3D SHAPES

You view Minecraft on a flat, two-dimensional screen, but the mobs, blocks, and world in Minecraft are three-dimensional. Understanding and visualizing this requires some imagination on your part.

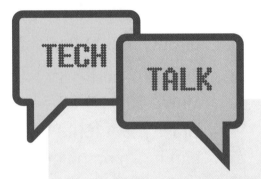

TWO-DIMENSIONAL, or **2D,** shapes have two dimensions. We usually call these length and width. 2D shapes are flat. This is a 2D chest.

THREE-DIMENSIONAL, or **3D,** shapes have three dimensions. We usually call these length, width, and height. 3D shapes are solid. This is a 3D chest.

Shape Sifter

Find and circle the five 3D shapes listed below.

CIRCLE	SQUARE	CYLINDER	RECTANGLE
PENTAGON	SQUARE-BASED PYRAMID	OCTAGON	SPHERE
CUBE	TRIANGLE	TRIANGULAR PRISM	HEXAGON

MINERAL HARDNESS

In Minecraft, some minerals are harder than others. The same is true in the real world. A *hardness scale*, where 1 is the softest and 10 is the hardest, is based on ten minerals. Geologists and mineralogists use this scale to classify the 3,800+ known minerals.

Hard, Harder, Hardest

The first (softest) mineral on the hardness scale is talc. It's where we get talcum powder. The last (hardest) mineral on the hardness scale is diamond.

Complete the puzzle challenge on the next page to put the other 8 minerals of this scale in order of hardness. Here are the rules: **BEGIN AT THE DOT BELOW EACH MINERAL NAME AND WORK YOUR WAY DOWN TO FIGURE OUT WHERE IN THE SCALE IT BELONGS.** *Every time you hit a horizontal line (one that goes across), you must follow it across to the next vertical line.*

Can you write the name of each mineral in its proper place on the scale?

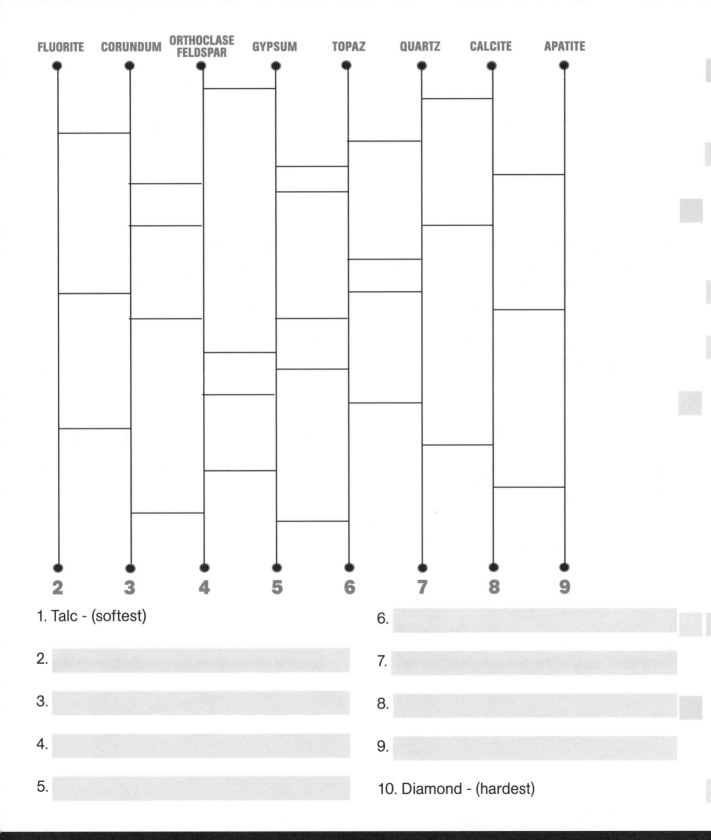

FLUORITE   CORUNDUM   ORTHOCLASE FELDSPAR   GYPSUM   TOPAZ   QUARTZ   CALCITE   APATITE

2   3   4   5   6   7   8   9

1. Talc - (softest)

2.

3.

4.

5.

6.

7.

8.

9.

10. Diamond - (hardest)

VIDEO GAME DESIGN

Video game designers use **STORYBOARDS** to plan how a game will flow. Each box contains a sketch of what will happen at each stage of the game. The boxes can be moved around, and new ones can be added to alter the game. Check out this storyboard for a trip to the Nether.

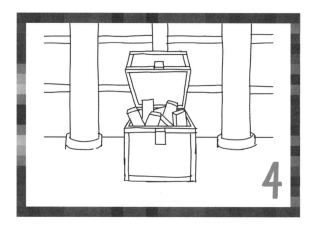

You Be the Designer!

Sketch a storyboard for an interactive Minecraft experience.

LIGHTNING ROD MATH

Lightning that strikes a house can do a lot of damage, ruining electronics or starting a fire. A metal pole, or lightning rod, placed on top of a building can conduct the energy from a strike to the ground, where it dissipates (spreads out and gradually disappears). **A LIGHTNING ROD IS A TOOL DESIGNED TO REDUCE DAMAGE FROM STORMS.**

Zombie Pigman Prevention

In Minecraft, a pig struck by lightning turns into a zombie pigman. In this puzzle, a lightning rod will protect every pig within 2 blocks horizontally, vertically, and diagonally. For example, every pig (shown as a red dot) is safe, protected by the lightning rod (shown as a yellow dot):

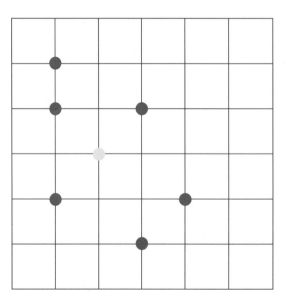

PLACE THREE YELLOW LIGHTNING RODS (YELLOW DOTS) ON THE GRID BELOW. Place them in such a way that they keep all the pigs safe during the next lightning storm. Remember that for a pig to be protected, it must be within 2 blocks of the rod.

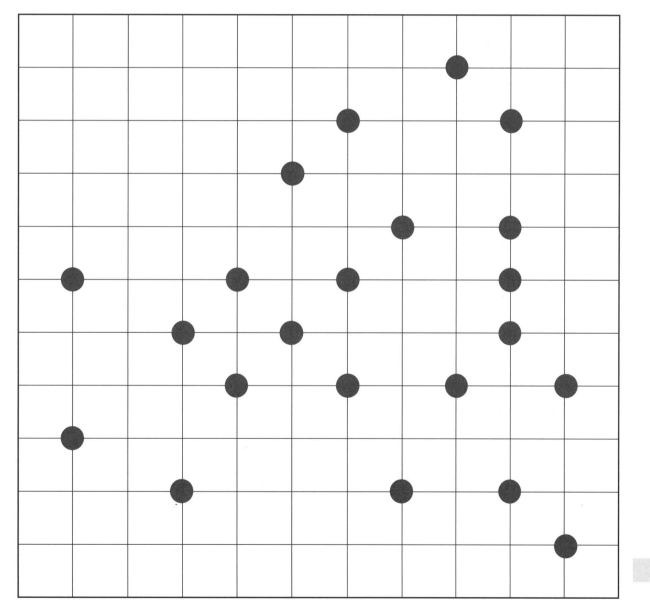

PREDICTING PATTERNS

Minecraft mobs are programmed to move and behave in certain ways. By observing how different mobs move, you discover patterns that help you predict how the mobs will move in the future.

Predicting a Mob's Moves

Meet Bat, whose movements in the game are programmed to follow these rules:

1) Bat will move as many as three squares at a time horizontally or vertically (not diagonally) in the direction he's facing.

2) If Bat runs into a **DOOR**, he's dead. Game over.

3) If Bat comes to a **WINDOW** (W), he opens it and keeps going in that direction until he meets another object.

4) If Bat meets with a **POTION** (P), he must turn right and can go another 3 squares.

5) If Bat runs into a **SPIDER** (S), he eats it and refuels. He can go another 3 squares in the same direction.

6) If Bat comes to a **CAVE**, he goes to sleep for the rest of the game. Zzzzz.

S	Bat ⮕		P
P	S	Cave	S
	Door		
P	S	W	P

USING WHAT YOU KNOW OF BAT'S MOVEMENTS, DRAW A LINE ON THE GRID ABOVE TO TRACE HIS PATH IN THE GAME. How does Bat's journey end?

Try this one! How does Bat's journey end?

	Door		P		S		P
S			W		Door		
		S				S	
W			P		← Bat		W
	W				S		S
Door			Cave		P		
	P			S			P
S			S			Door	

Observing Mob Patterns

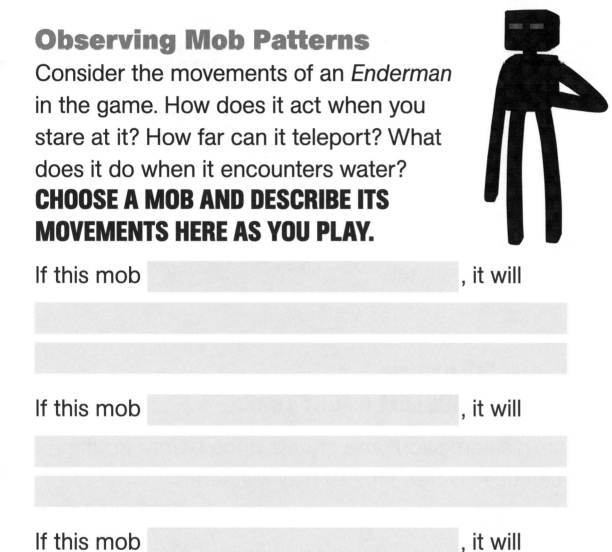

Consider the movements of an *Enderman* in the game. How does it act when you stare at it? How far can it teleport? What does it do when it encounters water? **CHOOSE A MOB AND DESCRIBE ITS MOVEMENTS HERE AS YOU PLAY.**

If this mob ＿＿＿＿＿＿＿＿＿＿＿＿＿＿＿, it will

＿＿＿＿＿＿＿＿＿＿＿＿＿＿＿＿＿＿＿＿＿＿

＿＿＿＿＿＿＿＿＿＿＿＿＿＿＿＿＿＿＿＿＿＿

If this mob ＿＿＿＿＿＿＿＿＿＿＿＿＿＿＿, it will

＿＿＿＿＿＿＿＿＿＿＿＿＿＿＿＿＿＿＿＿＿＿

＿＿＿＿＿＿＿＿＿＿＿＿＿＿＿＿＿＿＿＿＿＿

If this mob ＿＿＿＿＿＿＿＿＿＿＿＿＿＿＿, it will

＿＿＿＿＿＿＿＿＿＿＿＿＿＿＿＿＿＿＿＿＿＿

＿＿＿＿＿＿＿＿＿＿＿＿＿＿＿＿＿＿＿＿＿＿

How does knowing these patterns help you survive?

＿＿＿＿＿＿＿＿＿＿＿＿＿＿＿＿＿＿＿＿＿＿

＿＿＿＿＿＿＿＿＿＿＿＿＿＿＿＿＿＿＿＿＿＿

MATH GETS REAL

In the real world, we measure time by minutes, hours, days, years, etc. A day/night cycle lasts 24 hours.

In Minecraft, time is measured in ticks. An in-game day/night cycle lasts 24,000 ticks, which equals 20 real-world minutes.

Screen Time Dilemma
SOLVE THIS WORD PROBLEM ABOUT TIME.

If Keaton gets his homework and chores done before bedtime at 9:00, he can use his free time to play Minecraft.

He gets home from school at 3:30 and walks his dog for a half hour. He leaves at 4:00 for fencing practice and gets home 2 hours later. Dinner is at 6:00.

Keaton figures he needs an hour to do homework. Eating dinner takes half an hour, and it's his night to do dishes, so that's another half hour. He's got his shower down to twenty minutes before bed.

Will Keaton have time to play Minecraft? If so, how many in-game day/night cycles will he get to play?

_____

_____

Write your own Minecrafting word problem below. Challenge a friend or family member to solve it!

_____

_____

_____

_____

_____

_____

_____

_____

ARCHITECTURE: DRAWING TO SCALE

If a picture is drawn *to scale* or a model is built *to scale*, it means the drawing or model has the **SAME PROPORTIONS AS THE REAL-WORLD OBJECT, BUT IT'S SMALLER OR LARGER.** In math, art, construction, and elsewhere, the term *scale* represents the relationship between a measurement on a drawing or model and the corresponding measurement on a real-world object.

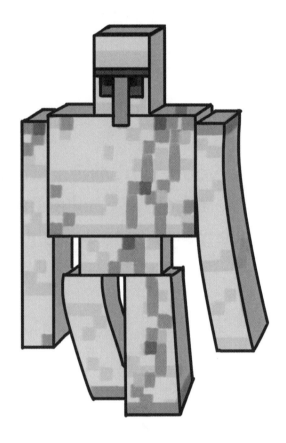

For example, 1 inch on a construction blueprint might represent 10 feet on a real-world house. One centimeter on a map might represent 18 real-world kilometers.

Supersize That Golem

Use the grid to copy the picture. Examine the lines in each small square in the smaller grid. Transfer those lines to the corresponding square in the large grid. Changing the size of the grid is one way to one way to increase scale and enlarge a drawing.

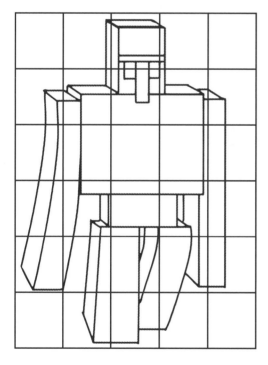

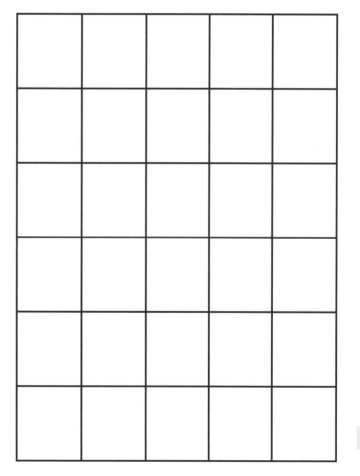

ALGORITHMS

An **ALGORITHM** is a set of steps to accomplish a task. If you give a friend directions to get from her house to yours, you create an algorithm. In computer science, an algorithm is **A SEQUENCE OF STEPS THE COMPUTER FOLLOWS TO SOLVE A PROBLEM OR BUILD A WORLD OR DO ANY OTHER TASK.** Learning to create algorithms will help you write computer programs.

WRITE AN ALGORITHM TO TELL A FRIEND HOW TO SOLVE A PROBLEM OR MAKE SOMETHING IN MINECRAFT.

How to

1.

2.

3.

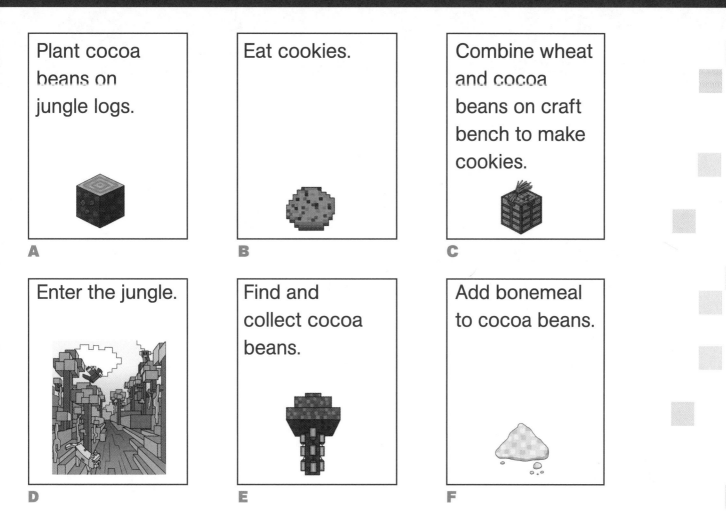

A
Plant cocoa beans on jungle logs.

B
Eat cookies.

C
Combine wheat and cocoa beans on craft bench to make cookies.

D
Enter the jungle.

E
Find and collect cocoa beans.

F
Add bonemeal to cocoa beans.

Order Up!

These scenes showing Minecraft activities are an algorithm for making cookies in Minecraft, but they are all mixed up. Can you put them in logical order from what happens first to what happens last?

Write the correct order of these scenes here:

___ ___ ___ ___ ___ ___

RUBE GOLDBERG MACHINES

Reuben Lucius "Rube" Goldberg (1883–1970) was an American cartoonist with a degree in engineering. He drew, invented, and built **WILDLY COMPLICATED MACHINES THAT DID SIMPLE TASKS.** His contraptions used common household objects connected in silly but logical ways.

Now, his work inspires artists, engineers, inventors, and many others.

Chain Reactions

Setting up a string of chain reactions is a way to build a Rube Goldberg Machine in Minecraft. Let's say the goal is to get a pig to drop a cooked pork chop. The process starts when you shoot an arrow at a wooden button. The process ends with a lava bucket setting a pig on fire and arrows firing from a dispenser, destroying the pig.

DESIGN YOUR OWN RUBE GOLDBERG MACHINE OF CAUSE AND EFFECT IN THE SPACE BELOW. Take it online and build, test, and improve your machine.

RUBE GOLDBERG MACHINES

What's the Point?

Solve this two-part puzzle. First, name the icons and figure out where each word goes in the crossword. The first word has been added for you. Second, transfer the numbered letters from the crossword to the numbered spaces at the bottom to reveal the purpose of a Rube Goldberg machine.

WATCH OUT SKELETON!

Crossword grid:
- 9 across (starts with handwritten M): M _ 4 _
- 6 across
- 3
- 7 12
- 5
- 8
- 2
- W (handwritten, above E of EVOKER)
- 1 E V O K E R 11
- 10 I (handwritten)
- 13 F (handwritten)

Bottom cipher:
_ _ _ _ _ _ _   E _ _ C _ _   _ _ C
6 9 2 12 6 7 6   1 13 13 5 11 3   13 5 11

_ _ _ _ _ _ I   C E _ I _ _
6 12 8 12 6 9 10   11 1 4 7 10 3 4

SIMPLE AND COMPLEX MACHINES

In science, **"WORK"** means using energy to apply a force to an object and move it some distance. A **SIMPLE MACHINE** is a device that makes work easier by changing the direction of or increasing the force. A **"SIMPLE MACHINE"** helps a person do the same amount of work with less effort.

Laugh Machine

The letters in the word **MACHINE** have been mixed in with the names of the six simple machines. Cross out the letters M-A-C-H-I-N-E in each row of letters, then write the remaining letters on the spaces. Finally, write the letters from the numbered boxes on the spaces with the same numbers to spell the answer to the joke.

What simple machine can cut the Minecraft ocean biome in half?

1. M A L E C H I V E N E R __ __ __ [1.] __

2. M A W C E D H I G E N E [2.] __ __ __ __ __ __

3. S M A C C R H I E N W E [3.] __ __ __ __ __ __

4. M A P U C H I L L E N E Y __ __ __ __ __ [4.] __

5. W H E M A C E H I L A N N D A X L E E

__ __ __ __ __ __ __ __ __ [5.] __ __ __

6. I N M A C L I N C H E D P I N L E A N E

__ __ __ __ __ __ __ __ __ __ __ [6.] __ __ __

__   __ __ __   __ __ __
5   3   1   4   3   6   2

WEATHER AND CLIMATE

Weather and climate are not the same things. **WEATHER** is what you have on any given day. **CLIMATE** is the weather of a region on Earth averaged over a long period of time.

Wither's Weather Words

Help the wither match the correct word to each clue and write the word in the boxes, as in a crossword.

ANEMOMETER	PRECIPITATION	TEMPERATE CLIMATE
BAROMETER	RAIN GAUGE	THERMOMETER
HYGROMETER	SATELLITE	WIND VANE

1. Water (in various forms) that falls to the ground

2. A tool in space that monitors weather and climate on Earth

3. A tool that measures wind speed

4. A tool that measures wind direction

5. A tool that measures atmospheric pressure (the force pushing on objects from the weight of the air above them)

6. A tool that collects and measures rainfall

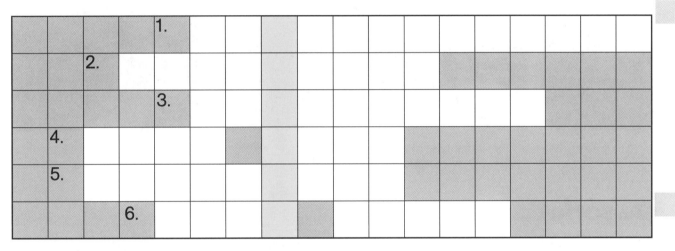

If you and the wither place the words correctly, the letters in the yellow column will spell the answer to this question:

What is the brightest light level you can enjoy in the game without worrying about snow and ice layers melting?

REAL BIOMES

Many Minecraft biomes are based on real-world climates.
BENEATH EACH ILLUSTRATION, WRITE THE LETTER PAIR FROM THE CLIMATE DESCRIPTION THAT BEST FITS THE BIOME PICTURED.

| jungle | ice plains | desert | extreme hills |

Descriptions

ES *Mountain climate:* Temperatures decrease with altitude, and high peaks are covered with snow.

AN *Temperate climate:* Warm and cold temperatures, no extremes, and rain through the year.

EC *Polar climate:* Cold temperatures all year and little precipitation.

IC *Tropical climate:* Warm temperatures all year and lots of rain.

OR *Desert climate:* Dry, very little rain, and extreme temperatures.

If you've matched the correct description to each picture, the letters will spell the answer to the question below. Can you separate the letters into the two-word answer?

WHAT DO SCIENTISTS STUDY IN ORDER TO LEARN WHAT THE EARTH WAS LIKE LONG AGO?

(Hint: They come from Antarctica.)

— — —   — — — — —

Check out the weather mods available for Minecraft online. You can add more dramatic storms, like hurricanes, to the game.

ANIMAL ADAPTATIONS

ADAPTATIONS are physical and behavioral traits that help animals survive. Having fur that matches an animal's environment is a common real-world adaptation. It provides **CAMOUFLAGE**, helping the animal blend with its surroundings. Prey animals with this adaptation can hide from predators, and predators can sneak up on prey without being noticed.

Minecraft rabbits usually have one of six different skins. ("Skins" are the textures used on the mobs.) What skin a rabbit has is determined by the biome where it spawns. For instance, 80% of rabbits in snowy biomes will be white, and 100% of rabbits in desert biomes will be gold.

Create a Creature

Invent an animal or mob and give it adaptations that allow it to thrive in one of the Minecraft biomes. What unique features help it find food and defend itself? Draw your creature below.

Adapt to Match

Many animals are adapted to match their environments. You need to adapt to reading backward to match the eight animals with one of their adaptations. Write the letter of the adaptation under the correct animal.

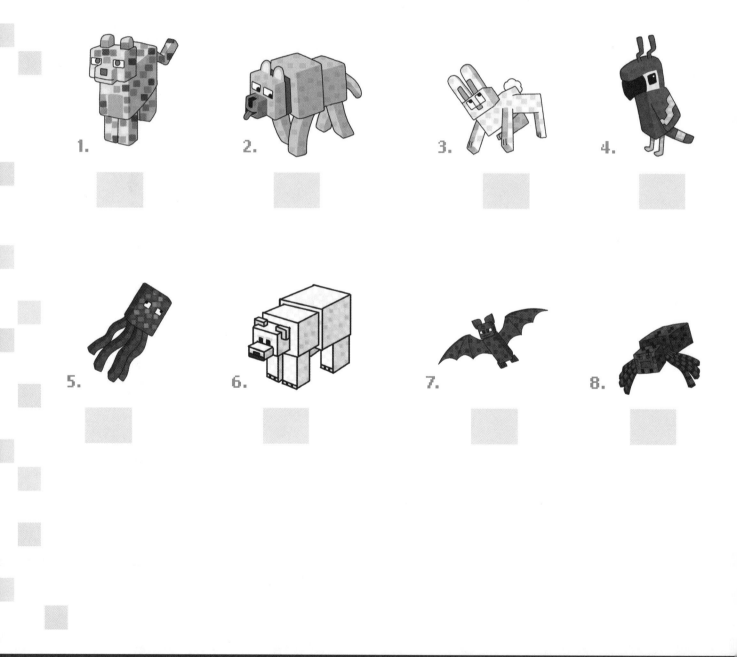

1.

2.

3.

4.

5.

6.

7.

8.

K. Yerp egral llik ot kcap a ni tnuh yeht.

F. Tnuh ot sbew dliub slamina eseht fo ynam.

I. Doof dnif ot dna yaw sti dnif ot noitacolohce sesu lamina siht.

H. Retaw gnidnuorrus duolc ot kni toohs nac lamina siht.

S. Mraw lamina citcra siht peek spleh taf fo reyal a.

E. Lamina siht looc pleh ecafrus eht ot esolc slessev doolb htiw srae gnol.

N. Senob ffo taem naelc lammam siht spleh repapdnas ekil eugnot a.

T. Sdees dna stun tae ti spleh lamina siht no kaeb devruc eht.

Use the letters you added to the grey boxes to fill in the answer to the riddle below!

Why is a giraffe's neck so long?

——— ——— ———   ——— ——— ——— ———   ——— ——— ——— ——— ———
 7   4   6   8   3   3   4   6   4   7   1   2

PLANT ADAPTATIONS

Some plants grow where it's hard to get food and sunlight and where they might be eaten by animals. **PLANTS ADAPT TO THEIR ENVIRONMENTS IN ORDER TO SURVIVE.** Some plants grow large, brightly colored, or scented flowers to attract pollinators. Some plants grow thorns so animals won't eat them. How do carnivorous, or meat-eating, plants survive? **RESEARCH THE VENUS FLYTRAP PLANT ONLINE AND WRITE ONE OR MORE FACTS ABOUT IT BELOW.**

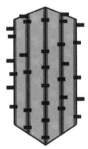

Meat-Eating Plant Mob

INVENT A CARNIVOROUS (MEAT-EATING) PLANT FOR MINECRAFT. Where will it spawn naturally? What animals will it eat? How will it trap its prey? How has it adapted to its environment? Draw and describe your plant here.

WORLDS WITHIN WORLDS

A Biome Like Mine

Minecraft has many biomes and creatures that inhabit them, just like in the real world. Consider the landscape and features of the town or area where you live. **INVENT A NEW MINECRAFT BIOME USING YOUR OWN SURROUNDINGS FOR INSPIRATION.**

Name of my biome:

1. What kind of terrain does your biome have?

2. What is the climate of your biome?

3. What resources are available?

4. What plants grow?

5. What animals do you encounter most?

6. How have the plants and animals adapted to this environment?

Draw and color a portion of your biome here. Include plants and animals.

RESOURCE MANAGEMENT

The real world has a limited supply of many natural resources, like fresh water, clean air, coal, and oil. **HUMANS ALL OVER THE PLANET ARE WORKING TO CONSERVE, OR SAVE, AVAILABLE RESOURCES AND FIND RENEWABLE RESOURCES**—like sun and wind power, fast-growing wood alternatives, and more—to replace the limited ones. Answer the questions below. Ask your parents for help if needed.

What are some ways you and your family conserve water?

What are some ways you and your family conserve energy?

Collecting Resources

It's harvest season; time to bring in the wheat. You want to be efficient and gather as much as possible. **DRAW A LINE FROM START TO STOP THAT PASSES THROUGH EVERY WHEAT ONCE AND ONLY ONCE.** Your line can go up, down, left, or right, but not diagonally. Ready, set, harvest!

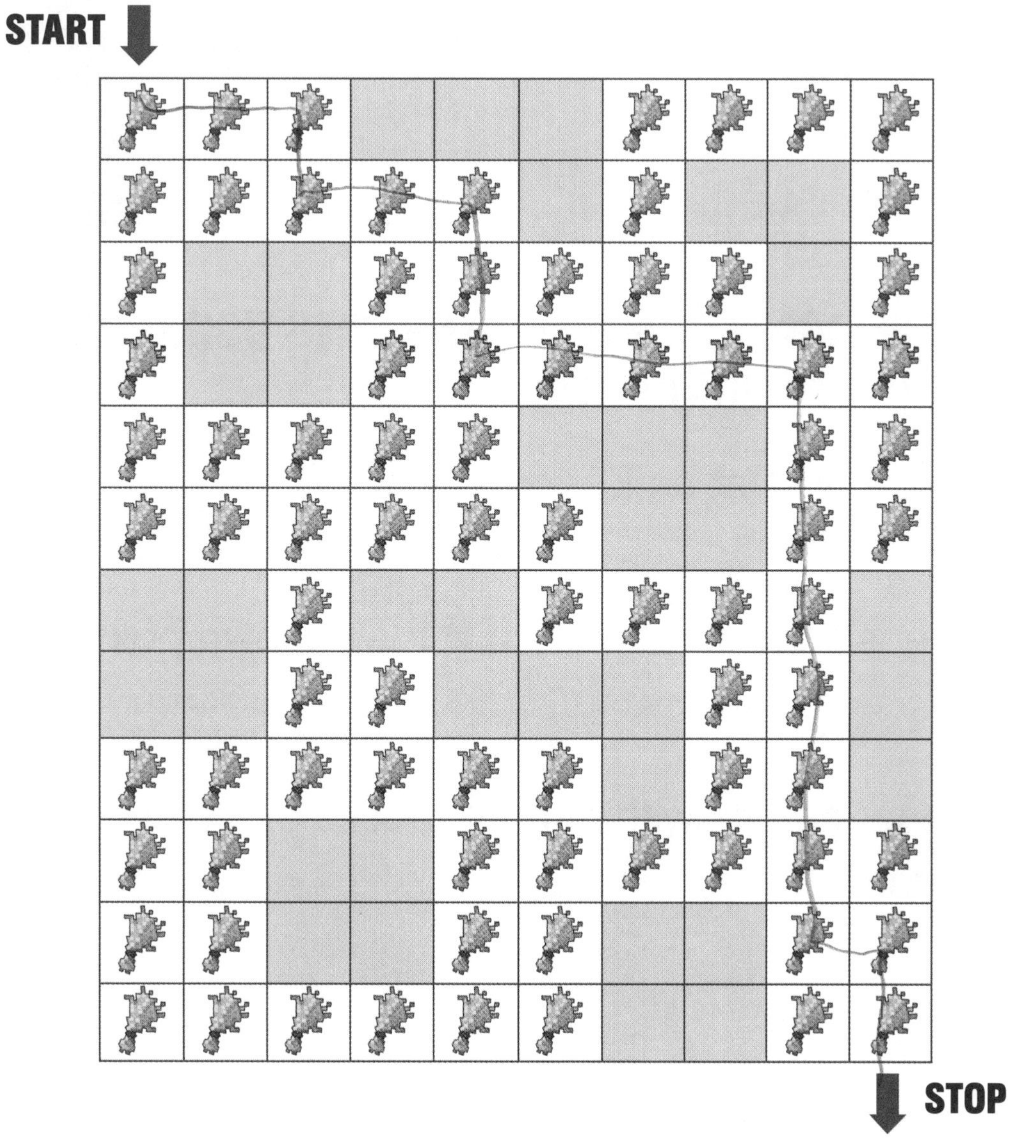

START

STOP

CONDITIONALS

Conditionals are if-then statements written into computer code that tell a program to do something only under certain conditions.

You make if-then decisions every day. If it's raining, you might wear a raincoat. If you finish your homework, you might get to play video games.

FINISH THESE CONDITIONAL STATEMENTS USING WHAT YOU KNOW ABOUT MINECRAFTING:

1. **IF** a player stares at an Enderman, **THEN** the Enderman will _____ .

2. **IF** a player sleeps in a bed, **THEN** their spawn point is _____ .

3. **IF** a creeper comes within three blocks of a player, **THEN** it will eventually _____ .

Only When If-Then

NEED SOMETHING FUN TO DO? TRY THIS MINECRAFTING CONDITIONALS GAME WITH TWO OR MORE PLAYERS.

1. If you've ever been killed by a skeleton in Minecraft, then yodel for 10 seconds.

2. If your shoes have laces, then tie the laces from the left shoe to the laces on the right shoe and proceed carefully to the closest door.

3. If you've ever worn a pumpkin on your head in Minecraft, then say the name of a pumpkin dessert in an Enderman voice.

4. If you've never built a redstone contraption, then do an impression of a creeper exploding.

5. If you have a first name that starts with a consonant, then spell Ender Dragon backward in a singing voice.

SPIDER WEBS

Spiders secrete silky threads used to engineer webs that trap prey. Spider threads are light, flexible, and surprisingly strong. They are comparable to steel and Kevlar (the stuff bulletproof vests are made of).

Web Challenge

HELP THE SPIDER NAVIGATE ITS WAY TO THE CENTER OF ITS STRONG WEB TO EAT ITS PREY.

Connecting Threads

Scientists use spider silk as a model to design medical devices and products that need to be flexible, light, strong, water-resistant, or sticky. Some of the items they've come up with so far are artificial tendons and ligaments, thread for stitches, adhesives, and bandages.

How would you use a lightweight, flexible, super-strong, water-resistant, sticky thread? **WHAT INVENTIONS COULD YOU MAKE WITH SPIDER SILK, AND WHAT EVERYDAY PROBLEMS COULD YOU SOLVE?** Write your ideas here.

GENETICS

INHERITED TRAITS ARE CHARACTERISTICS PASSED FROM PARENTS TO OFFSPRING. ALL ORGANISMS INHERIT TRAITS FROM THEIR PARENTS. Some characteristics to look for in animals are body structure, skin texture, fur color, and shapes of eyes, ears, noses, and faces. Family members share many traits, which is why they often look similar.

An *animal never gets a trait from just one parent.* Rather, every trait gets input from both parents. So even though a piglet has a crooked tail like her father, she got genetic input for her tail from both her mother and father.

Mob Babies

Below are sets of mob parents with different characteristics that their baby can inherit. **DRAW THEIR BABY IN THE BOXES PROVIDED USING TRAITS AND GENETIC INPUT FROM BOTH PARENTS.** For example, choose your baby zombie's eye color based on its parents' eye colors.

BONES

Minecraft skeletons drop bones. Thankfully, your skeleton does not!

Bones are part of the skeletal system. **ANIMALS THAT HAVE BONES, INCLUDING HUMANS, ARE CALLED VERTEBRATES.** Bones serve many functions. Some protect soft, fragile parts of the body. For example, your skull protects your brain. Other bones help you move, like the bones in your arms and legs, which support muscle.

Know Your Bones

Your body has over 200 bones, but only 10 have been dropped here. **CAN YOU CIRCLE ALL 10 BONE NAMES IN THE CHART BELOW?**

Cranium	Mandible	Vertebrae	Clavicle	Navel
Sternum	Ribs	Pelvis	Cartilage	Teeth
Liver	Femur	Nostril	Tibia	Fibula

No Bones About It

THESE 10 STATEMENTS ARE EITHER TRUE OR FALSE. YOU DECIDE. If you think a statement is true, circle the letter in the T column. If you think it's false, circle the letter in the F column.

1.	T	F	Most people have 12 ribs, but a few (very few) have 13.
2.	T	F	The biggest joint in your body is your shoulder.
3.	T	F	Your body has 206 bones.
4.	T	F	More than half your bones are in your hands and feet.
5.	T	F	Bone marrow, in the middle of most bones, is stiff and hard as steel.
6.	T	F	The smallest bone in your body is the stapes in the ear.
7.	T	F	The largest bone in your body is the humerus in your upper arm.
8.	T	F	Only about 10% of Earth's animals have bones.
9.	T	F	Human babies are born with twice as many bones as you have.
10.	T	F	Broken bones repair themselves.

MAGNETS

MAGNETISM is a force all around you. You can't see it, but you can see what it does. Magnets exert a force, attracting certain metals, particularly iron, nickel, and cobalt.

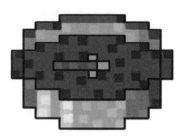

MAGNETS come in different shapes, such as bars, horseshoes, and rings. Each has two poles, called **NORTH** and **SOUTH.** North and south poles (opposite poles) are attracted to each other, while two north poles or two south poles (like poles) repel each other.

Magnet Magic Trick

Magnets are so fun and fascinating that they're used in many magic tricks. Here's one you can try. **IMPRESS YOUR FRIENDS BY MAKING ONE PAPERCLIP MAGICALLY (OR MAGNETICALLY) STICK TO ANOTHER.** You need two metal paperclips and a small (but strong enough) magnet you can hide behind a finger or two.

1. Hold one curved end of a paperclip between your thumb and one or two fingers of one hand. Also hold the magnet between these same fingers, pressed against the paperclip. Keeping the magnet hidden can be tricky. You'll need to practice.

2. With your other hand, place the second paperclip so it's barely touching the exposed end of the first one. The force of the magnet will attract the second paperclip to the first and hold it there. Impressive!

Now challenge your friends to do the same—but don't give them the magnet!

Stuck!

This iron golem is magnetized. As he wanders around the village path he's on, magnetic objects stick to him. **CIRCLE THE ITEMS THAT ARE MOST LIKELY TO STICK TO HIM.** Remember, a magnetic force works over a distance, so he doesn't have to be touching an item to have it attract and stick.

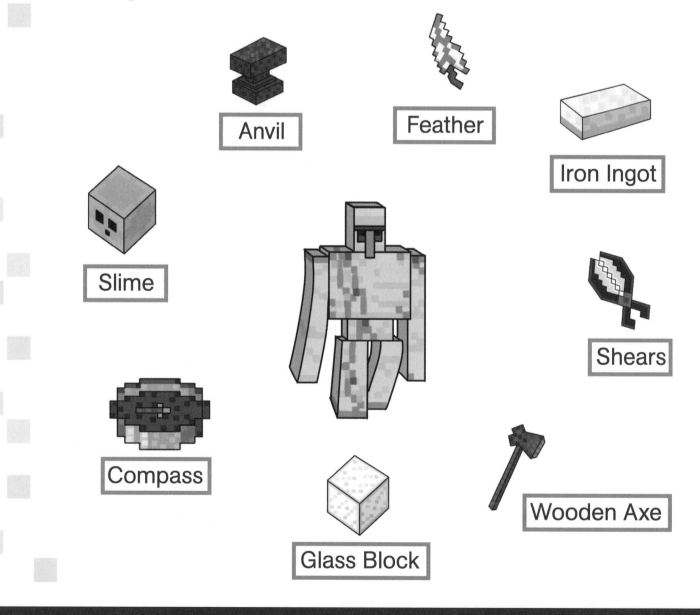

Anvil

Feather

Iron Ingot

Slime

Shears

Compass

Glass Block

Wooden Axe

SOUND

Sound is a vibration that travels through air, water, or solid matter and can be heard.

WHEN AN OBJECT VIBRATES, IT MOVES THE AIR AROUND IT, MAKING PARTICLES IN THE AIR VIBRATE, TOO. The vibrating particles close to the object cause the particles next to them to vibrate, and on and on, farther away from the original vibrating object. This flow of the vibration away from the object is called a wave.

THINK OUTSIDE THE BOOK

Try this experiment to see the effects of sound waves. Stretch plastic wrap tightly over a bowl and secure it with a rubber band. Sprinkle pepper on top of the plastic. With permission and care, bang a metal pot loudly with a metal spoon near the bowl. Watch the pepper closely. What happens? Why do you think it happens?

Sound Words

A piston hits each of the letter strings below from the left-hand side, causing a chain reaction, like a wave. When the piston hits the first letter, it changes the letter to the one that follows it in the alphabet. The change in the first letter causes a change in the letter next to it, and on and on. The wave travels through the whole word, changing each of the letters in turn.

CAN YOU IDENTIFY THE SOUND WORDS THAT THE PISTON CHANGED? (Note: The letter Z changes to an A when it's hit by a wave.)

U N K T L D = ___ ___ ___ ___ ___ ___

O H S B G = ___ ___ ___ ___ ___

D B G N = ___ ___ ___ ___

D Z Q C Q T L = ___ ___ ___ ___ ___ ___ ___

U N B Z K B G N Q C R = ___ ___ ___ ___ ___

___ ___ ___ ___ ___ ___

WATCH OUT! An evoker rolled the letters below to the ones that come before them in the alphabet. The correct letters spell the answer to this joke. **DECODE THE ANSWER.**

What did the skeleton say when the bat squeaked in her ear?

P V D I !   U I B U   N F H B I F S U A !

__ __ __ __! __ __ __ __

__ __ __ __ __ __ __ __ __ __ __

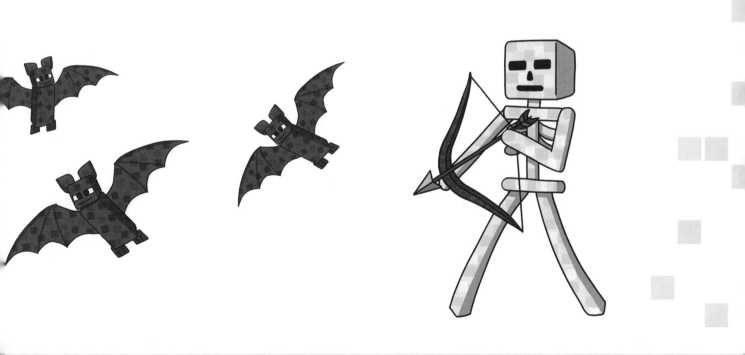

MAKING WAVES

SLAM

Facts about Minecraft's sounds are coming at you on the waves below. **READ EVERY OTHER LETTER ON THE WAVE TO DECIPHER THE MESSAGES.**

Minecraft's music and sound-effect producer is

D W A R N O I N E G L O R T O R S Y E A N G F A E I L N D

_ _ _ _ _ _   _ _ _ _ _ _ _ _

Originally, he wanted to be

A O S M T S U S N O T B C O A R R E D H R R I E V P E U R S

_ _____ ___ _____

His Minecraft skin is the default skin with this one change:

A R J A U T K O E E B L O A X M H A E L A L D

_ _____ ____

Ghast sounds are made by

D D A L N R I O E W L D S L C I A U T

_____ ' ___

FOSSILS

Remains of ancient life are preserved in rocks as fossils. **THESE FOSSILS PROVIDE INFORMATION ABOUT THE ORGANISMS AND ENVIRONMENTAL CONDITIONS FROM MILLIONS AND BILLIONS OF YEARS AGO.** They are also evidence of evolution.

Conditions have to be just right for fossils to form, so very few organisms become fossilized. It happens when an animal is buried by sediment (mud, volcanic ash, sand, etc.) soon after it dies. Layer upon layer of sediment builds up. The animal's soft tissues decompose quickly, but the bones remain. Gradually, the bones are replaced by rock minerals, which are the fossils you see in museums. **AS EARTH'S TECTONIC PLATES SHIFT, LAYERS OF ROCK THAT ENCASE FOSSILS ARE PUSHED TO THE SURFACE.**

DID YOU KNOW?

Erosion from wind, rain, and rivers can expose fossils near the surface, as can people who dig and look for them.

Fossil Match

FOSSILS TELL US A LOT ABOUT A CREATURE'S BONE STRUCTURE, and every kind of animal has a unique bone structure. Match each forearm to the correct animal. Write the number in the blank line.

1. Bird

2. Lion

3. Human

4. Frog

5. Horse

6. Whale

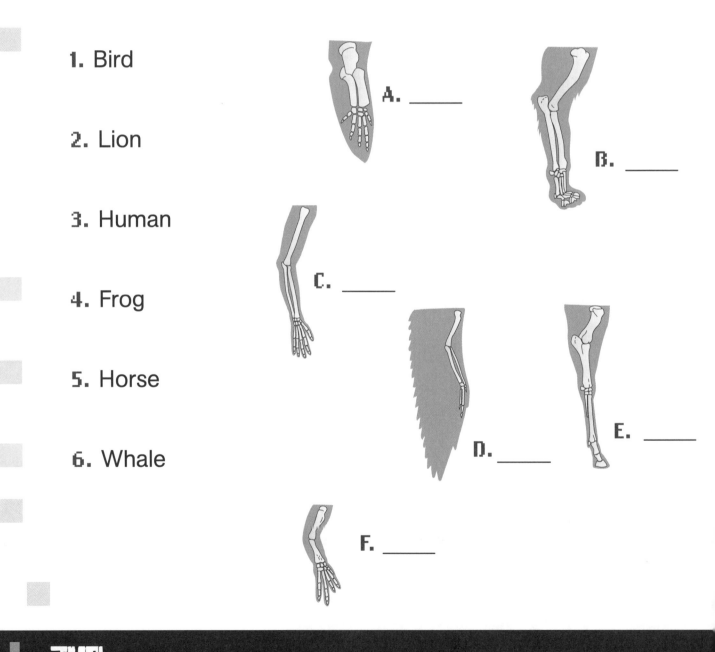

A. _____

B. _____

C. _____

D. _____

E. _____

F. _____

THINK OF YOUR FAVORITE MONSTER OR MOB IN MINECRAFT. WHAT WOULD ITS FOSSIL LOOK LIKE? DRAW IT HERE:

ANSWERS

PAGE 192-193
THE PHYSICS OF FORCE

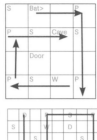

PAGE 195, SHAPE SIFTER

CIRCLE	SQUARE	CYLINDER	RECTANGLE
PENTAGON	SQUARE BASED PYRAMID	OCTAGON	SPHERE
CUBE	TRIANGLE	TRIANGULAR PRISM	HEXAGON

PAGE 197, MINERAL HARDNESS
Hard, Harder, Hardest
1. Talc
2. Gypsum
3. Calcite
4. Fluorite
5. Apatite
6. Orthoclase Feldspar
7. Quartz
8. Topaz
9. Corundum
10. Diamond

PAGE 199, VIDEO GAME DESIGN
Answers may vary.

PAGE 201, LIGHTNING ROD MATH

PAGE 203-205, PREDICTING PATTERNS
Predicting a Mob's Moves
1.

2.

Observing Mob Patterns
Answers may vary.

PAGE 206, MATH GETS REAL
Screen Time Dilemma
Keaton has 5½ hours (330 minutes) from the time he gets home from school to the time he goes to bed. He walks his dog for 30 minutes, spends 2 hours (120 minutes) at fencing practice, ½ hour (30 minutes) eating dinner, ½ hour (30 minutes) doing dishes, 1 hour doing homework (60 minutes), and 20 minutes showering. That's 4 hours and 50 minutes (290 minutes) used for chores and activities. Yes, Keaton does have time to play Minecraft. Keaton has 40 minutes to play Minecraft, for 2 in-game day/night cycles.

PAGE 210-211, ALGORITHMS
Order Up!
D, E, A, F, C, B

Write an Algorithm
Answers may vary.

PAGE 215, RUBE GOLDBERG MACHINES
What's the Point?
Maximum effort for minimal results

		G			
Z	H	U	⁴S	K	
O	⁹A				
⁶M	S	Q	⁷U	¹²I	D
B	A	³T		⁵O	
I				⁸N	
V	E	²X	W	K	
	¹E	V	O	K	E	¹R
		¹⁰L		Y	
		¹³F			

PAGE 217, SIMPLE AND COMPLEX MACHINES
Laugh Machine
Lever, Wedge, Screw, Pulley, Wheel and Axle, Inclined Plane
What simple machine can cut a Minecraft ocean biome in half?
A See Saw (a sea saw, get it?)

PAGE 219, WEATHER AND CLIMATE
Wither's Weather Words
Eleven is the highest light level you can enjoy without snow and ice layers melting.

PAGE 221, REAL BIOMES
What do scientists study in order to learn what the earth was like long ago? (Hint: They come from Antarctica.) ICE CORES

Ice cores are cylinders drilled out of the Antarctic ice. It's like the tube of slush you get when you stick a straw into a slushy drink, put your finger on the top of the straw, and then pull the straw out. Scientists have drilled ice cores from two miles below the surface where the ice was formed a long time ago. By studying the old ice, we can learn what the climate was like when that ice formed.

PAGE 224, ANIMAL ADAPTATIONS
Adapt to Match
1. N, 2. K, 3. E, 4. T, 5. H, 6. S, 7. I, 8. F
Why is a giraffe's neck so long?
Its feet stink

PAGE 227, PLANT ADAPTATIONS
Answers may vary.

PAGE 229, WORLDS WITHIN WORLDS
A Biome Like Mine
Answers will vary.

PAGE 230-231, RESOURCE MANAGEMENT
Answer may vary. Some answers may include:
What are some ways that you and your family conserve water?
Turning off the water while you brush your teeth.
Taking shorter showers.
Using rain barrels to collect water.

What are some ways that you and your family conserve energy?
Turning off the lights when you're not using them.
Using solar-powered lights or adding solar panels to your home.
Using energy-efficient lightbulbs in your home.

Collection Resources

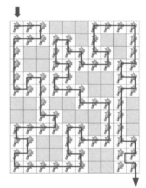

PAGE 232-233, CONDITIONALS
1. If a player stares at an Enderman, then the Enderman will teleport toward the player and attack it.
2. If a player sleeps in a bed, then their spawn point is set at that location.
3. If a creeper comes within three blocks of a player, then it will eventually explode!

PAGE 234, SPIDER WEBS
Web Challenge

PAGE 235,
CONNECTING THREADS
Answers will vary.

PAGE 237, GENETICS
Answers will vary.

PAGE 238-239, BONES
Know Your Bones
Cranium
Mandible
Vertebrae
Clavicle
Sternum
Ribs
Pelvis
Femur
Tibia
Fibula

No Bones About It
1. T, 2. F, 3. T, 4. T, 5. F, 6. T, 7. F, 8. T, 9. F, 10. T

PAGE 242, MAGNETS
Stuck
Circle the following items:
Anvil, Iron Ingot, Shears, Compass.

PAGE 244-245, SOUND
Think Outside the Book
Banging the pot creates sound vibrations that cause the pepper to bounce or move.

Sound Words
Volume: how loud or quiet a sound is
Pitch: the lowness or highness of sound
Echo: sound waves that bounce off objects
Eardrum: sound waves cause this membrane in the ear to vibrate
Vocal chords: these vibrate when a person talks or a cat purrs

What did the skeleton say when the bat squeaked in her ear?
Ouch! That megahertz!

A hertz (Hz) measures wave frequency. One hertz is one wave cycle per second. A megahertz (MHz) is 1,000,000 cycles per second. The average human ear detects sounds between 20 and 20,000 Hz. Sound waves around 20 Hz are low-pitched, *bass* frequencies. Sound waves above 5,000 Hz are high-pitched, *treble* frequencies, like Minecraft bat squeaks. Did you notice that people can't hear frequencies above 20,000 Hz? That means you can't hear sound from waves that are 1,000,000 Hz (or 1 MHz.) Radio waves are measured in MHz.

PAGE 246, MAKING WAVES
Daniel Rosenfeld
A stunt car driver
A jukebox head
Daniel's cat

PAGE 248, FOSSILS
Fossil Match
1. D
2. B
3. C
4. F
5. E
6. A

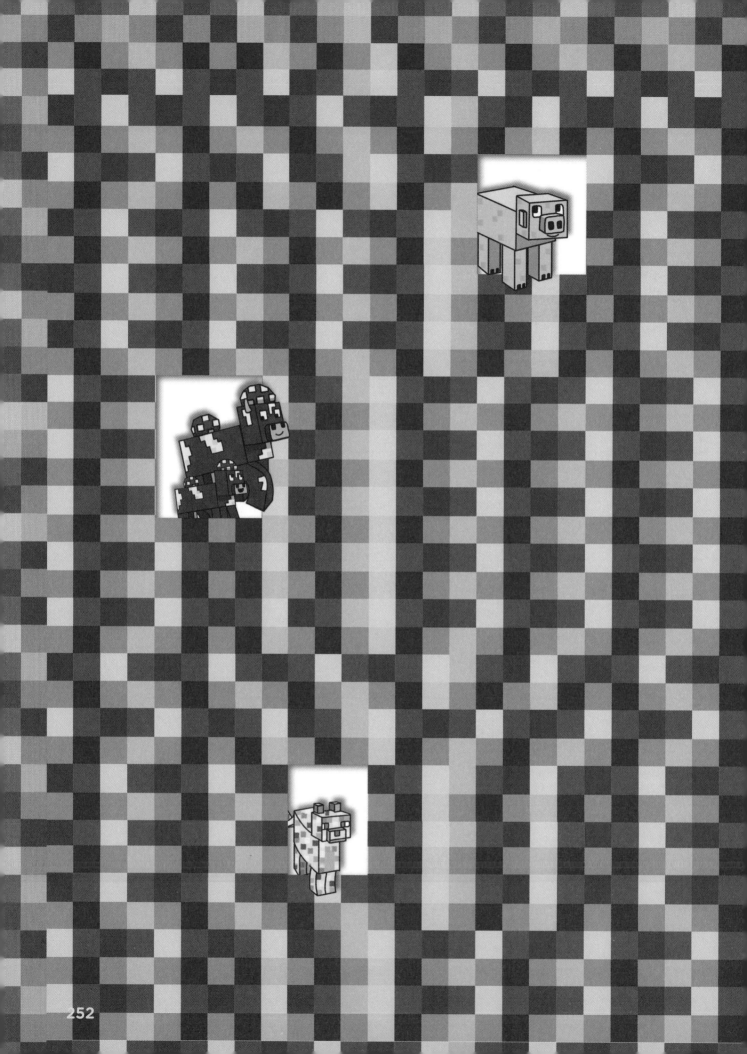

CHAPTER FIVE

LEARNING ADVENTURES IN READING, WRITING, MATH, AND SCIENCE

CONTENTS

WORD JUMBLE

Write the words in the correct order so that the sentence makes sense. Don't forget to capitalize the first word in the sentence and add a period at the end.

1. a profession with Nitwit is no villager

_____

_____

2. used fish are fishing tools to catch rods

_____

_____

3. the job of the Ender Dragon is the Ender crystal to heal

_____

_____

4. the zombie pit fell into it and a player built the lava

_____

_____

READING WORDS

Draw a line to match each word to the picture.

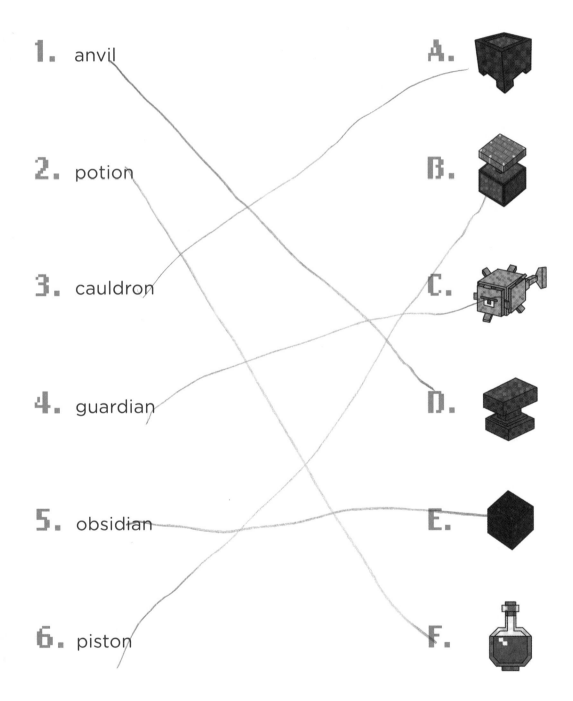

1. anvil

2. potion

3. cauldron

4. guardian

5. obsidian

6. piston

A.

B.

C.

D.

E.

F.

RHYMING WORDS

Use the rhyming words to complete the sentences. Don't forget to capitalize the first word in the sentence.

bee	cow	ditch	gears	habit	pen
plow	rabbit	shears	ten	tree	witch

1. The _____ built its hive in a _____.

2. _____ pigs were in the _____.

3. The _____ pulled a _____ through the wheat field.

4. The _____ had a _____ of twitching its nose.

5. Steve cut the _____ with the _____.

6. The _____ used a pickaxe to build a _____ around its house.

257

PREFIXES

Draw a line from the prefix to a base word and write the new word on the line. Hint: Use each prefix and base word only once.

Prefix	Base Word	New Word
1. un	possible	
2. re	view	
3. pre	behave	
4. im	agree	
5. mis	school	
6. dis	seen	

PREFIXES

Add a prefix to each bolded base word to form a new word that fits the definition.

I am **un**happy.

Prefixes

re – again	dis – opposite of	mis – incorrect
un – not	under – below	pre – before

Word	Definition
1. _____	to **view** again
2. _____	below **water**
3. _____	**spell** incorrectly
4. _____	**heat** before
5. _____	not **happy**
6. _____	opposite of **agree**

SUFFIXES

Add suffixes to the base words to form new words. Write the words under the suffix. The first one is done for you.

Bat is creep**y**.

excite	friend	dirt	child	care
wind	agree	noise	kind	retire	like

1. -ment

excitement

agreement

retirement

2. -y

3. -ish

4. -ness

5. -ly

6. -ship

SUFFIXES

Use the spelling rules to add the suffix to the base word.

Skeleton is run**ning**.

If a word ends in a short vowel and consonant, double the consonant before adding the suffix.	run ➞	running
If a word ends in a silent e, drop the e before adding the suffix.	hope ➞	hoping
If a word ends with a consonant y, change the y to i before adding the suffix.	happy ➞	happiness
If a word ends with a vowel y, just add the suffix.	joy ➞	joyful

1. hug + ing _____

2. jump + ed _____

3. slip + ed _____

4. slide + ing _____

5. hop + ing _____

6. dig + ing _____

7. beauty + ful _____

8. smile + ed _____

9. care + ing _____

10. cut + ing _____

PREFIXES AND SUFFIXES

Underline the prefix and circle the suffix in each word. Draw a line from the word to its meaning.

1. unforgettable

2. indescribable

3. misspelling

4. unfriendly

5. unhelpful

6. uncontrollable

A. not able to be described

B. not like a friend

C. not full of help

D. not able to be controlled

E. not able to forget

F. incorrect spelling

DIVIDING SYLLABLES

Draw a line between the syllables of each word. The first one is done for you.

Rules for Dividing Syllables

Divide between compound words	book/shelf
Divide between two consonant letters	zom/bie
Prefixes and suffixes are syllables	creep/er
Divide after the long vowel	ro/bot
Divide after the consonant following a short vowel	Al/ex

1. black/smith

2. danc/ing

3. zom/bie

4. villag/er

5. butter/fly

6. cob/web

7. emer/alds

8. Ender/man

LEARNING NEW WORDS

Read the clues. Answer the questions.

1. In the real world, **elytra** are the wings of a beetle. In

Minecraft, elytra help the players do what?

A. attack   (B. fly)

2. In the real world, **diorite** is a speckled rock. In Minecraft,

a diorite block is used for what?

(A. to make granite)   B. for food

3. In the real world, a **portal** is a doorway or entrance.

In Minecraft, the Nether portal is used as what?

(A. a gateway between the Overworld and the Nether)

B. a boat to travel on water

4. In the real world, a **default** is given by the computer.

In Minecraft, who is a default player?

(A. Steve)   B. Creeper

5. In the real world, a **piston** moves fluid in an engine.

In Minecraft a piston does what?

A. grinds up other blocks   (B. moves other blocks)

DETERMINE MEANING OF WORDS

Read the sentences. Use the context clues to determine the meaning of the underlined words. Circle the best meaning.

I love to learn new words!

1. Steve and Alex thought the joke was so <u>hilarious</u> that they couldn't stop laughing.

   A. rude   **(B. funny)**

2. Steve had <u>insufficient</u> diamond blocks, so he could not make a sword.

   (A. not enough)   B. too many

3. Iron golem will not <u>permit</u> Evoker into a village.

   (A. let or allow)   B. protect or keep out

4. Creeper became <u>outraged</u> and exploded on the player.

   A. happy   **(B. angry)**

5. The Arctic Biome is <u>barren</u>, with few plants and animals.

   (A. without life)   B. with lots of life

DICTIONARY GUIDEWORDS

Read the guidewords at the top of each page. Then write the words in the box on the correct page.

Guidewords are the two words at the top of each dictionary page. All the words on the page of a dictionary come between the two words alphabetically.

potato	goat	bread	moon	flower	lava	carrot	butterfly
iron	apple	clock	magma	ocelot	emerald	lever	orb

1.

anvil   cat

_____

_____

_____

_____

2.

chicken   hug

_____

_____

_____

_____

3.

ink   melon

_____

_____

_____

_____

4.

minecart   rabbit

_____

_____

_____

_____

MULTIPLE MEANING WORDS

Read the sentence. Then circle the letter of the meaning that matches the underlined word.

1. The chickens were making a <u>racket</u>.
   A. a type of bat   B. a loud noise

2. The creeper will <u>charge</u> at the player.
   A. the cost of something   B. attack

3. The parrot's <u>bill</u> is black.
   A. an amount of money owed   B. the beak of a bird

4. The sunken <u>ship</u> was at the bottom of the ocean.
   A. a large boat   B. to send a package

5. Alex is trying to <u>train</u> pig.
   A. to teach   B. railroad cars

6. You can <u>change</u> the skins on your player.
   A. to make different   B. coins

HOMOPHONES

Read each sentence. Write the homophones on the lines to complete the sentence in a way that makes sense.

Homophones are words that sound the same but are spelled differently and have different meanings.

1. Horse _____ _____ carrots. ~~eight~~/~~ate~~

2. When cows _____ a creeper and die, they drop _____ . meat/meet

3. Steve _____ how to find the _____ entrance to the cave. new/knew

4. Creepers _____ that _____ mob can survive their explosion. know/no

5. Creepers will drop _____ heads over _____ when _____ dying. their/they're/there

6. Those _____ creepers are _____ tired _____ play. two/to/too

MORE HOMOPHONES

Circle the homophones in the puzzle.

Which witch?

blew/blue	whole/hole	weight/wait	road/rode	sea/see
peace/piece	knight/night	break/brake	wood/would	tale/tail

```
K N I G H T Z Y E R S N R W
N E T H G I E W C L O E D T
J B U Y J L R W A L O A A D
N G R L I Y D H E Y D H D Q
K T B A B R N O P P R T V R
M A T K K Z T L P E H E E S
D J E W Y E X E C G B W R J
R R N R X R L E I W E O Z T
W A I T B L I N O L D Q J T
D E J R T P T U B E Y L T N
O J L V D V L V Z Q M R T L
O K R A K D D B D R B X V D
W Q V J T J L T N G Y K B N
```

ON THE FARM

Read about Steve's adventure on the farm. Write the nouns on the lines. Circle all the proper nouns.

Nouns name people, places, things, or events. A **proper noun** names a one-of-a-kind noun. Proper nouns always begin with a capital letter.

Steve enjoys being on the farm. He likes to feed the animals. He likes to breed them too. The cows and sheep like to eat wheat. The pigs like to eat carrots or beetroots. The chickens like to eat seeds. Two animals will have a baby. Babies grow up in 20 minutes. Steve has to build lots of pens to keep the animals safe. He also builds a barn and a coop.

CREEPER ACTION

Choose a verb to complete each sentence. Write the verb in its correct form.

Verbs

run	explode	hiss	flash	attack	climb

1. Creeper _____ loudly when it saw the player.

2. Creeper will _____ any player within 16 blocks.

3. When creeper attacks, it _____.

4. Creeper can _____ ladders and vines.

5. Creeper _____ away from ocelots and cats.

6. Creeper _____ before it explodes.

ORDERING ADJECTIVES

Write adjectives on the lines to describe each picture. Use each adjective only once.

Adjectives

white	pink	yellow	green	five
creepy	long	cute	spotted	old

1. Ocelot is a _____ _____ cat.

2. Chicken laid _____ _____ eggs.

3. Nitwit wears _____ _____ clothing.

4. The _____ _____ house was haunted.

5. Alex tamed the _____ _____ pig.

ADVERBS

Underline the verb in the sentence once and the adverb twice. The first one is done for you.

> An **adverb** describes an action verb. It tells how, when, or where and action happens.

1. Creeper <u>hissed</u> <u><u>loudly</u></u>.

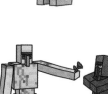

2. Iron golem <u><u>awkwardly</u></u> handed the flower to the villager.

3. Alex <u><u>gently</u></u> cared for the animals.

4. The baby zombie villagers played <u><u>happily</u></u>.

5. Alex <u><u>carefully</u></u> put the diamond armor in the chest.

6. The bee <u>buzzed</u> <u><u>quickly</u></u> from flower to flower.

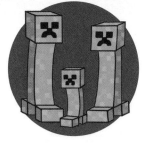

CONJUNCTIONS

Write the conjunction that best completes the sentence.

Conjunctions

and	or	but	so

1. Bees __and__ bats have wings.

2. Chickens can swim, __but__ baby chickens cannot.

3. Is that a shulker __or__ a purpur block?

4. Witches can drink __or__ throw potions.

5. Blaze is a fiery mob __but__ be careful not to get burned.

6. A donkey can be controlled __but__ first it must be tamed.

PREPOSITIONS

Complete each sentence using the correct preposition.

Prepositions

on   in   around   under   behind   over

1. The diamond armor is _____in_____ the chest.

2. Steve is _____behind_____ the cow.

3. The carrot is _____on_____ the stick.

4. The creepers are dancing _____under_____ the disco ball.

5. Alex's arm is _____over_____ cow.

6. Bat flew _____around_____ the tree.

PREPOSITIONAL PHRASES

Circle the preposition and underline the prepositional phrase in each sentence. The first one is done for you.

1. Steve collected wood (from) <u>the forest</u> to build a shelter.

2. Steve climbed up a tree to get away from the mobs.

3. You can find a witch hut in the Swampland Biome.

4. Inside the witch hut, you can find a crafting table.

5. Horses can be found in the Plains Biome.

6. If you click on a horse, you can ride it.

PARTS OF A SENTENCE

Underline the subject once and the predicate twice. The first one is done for you.

> The **subject** of a sentence tells who or what the sentence is about.
>
> The **predicate** of a sentence tells what the subject is or does.

1. The Minecraft world has many mobs.

2. You can tame some mobs.

3. Some mobs can be eaten.

4. Creeper likes to screech and explode.

5. Utility mobs can help a player.

6. Iron golem is a utility mob.

FRAGMENTS AND SENTENCES

*Write **S** if the group of words is a sentence. Write **F** if the group of words is a fragment.*

A **sentence** has a subject and a predicate.

A **fragment** is missing a subject or a predicate.

1. A passive mob will never attack a player. _____

2. A neutral mob like wolves and spiders. _____

3. Snow golem and iron golem are utility mobs. _____

4. An aggressive mob will attack on sight. _____

5. Looking to kill players. _____

6. Fun to interact with in the Minecraft world. _____

COMPOUND SENTENCES

Use a comma and a coordinating conjunction to combine the two sentences into one compound sentence. The first one is done for you.

Coordinating Conjunctions

| and | or | but | so |

1. Steve found a diamond. He put it in his cart.

   Steve found a diamond, so he put it in his cart.

2. Steve wanted to tame a creeper. It exploded.

   _____

3. Steve can go to the Desert Biome. He can go to the Jungle Biome.

   _____

4. Steve likes to play in the village. Alex likes to play on the farm.

   _____

PUNCTUATION AND CAPITALIZATION

Write each sentence on the line, adding capitals and punctuation.

1. zombies are undead hostile mobs

_____

2. watch out for baby zombies

_____

3. baby zombies are even more dangerous than big zombies

_____

4. on halloween, zombies put pumpkins on their heads

_____

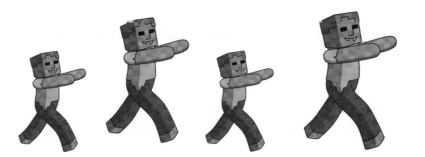

EDITING

Steve wrote a report about the venomous cave spider.
Use the editing marks to correct the mistakes.

∧   insert word

⤸ℓ   delete word

⊙   add period

⋏   insert comma

sp. ⬭   correct spelling

≡   capitalize

Cave Spiders

Cave spiders live abandoned mineshafts they climb walls

and hid in cobwebs. The all so swim so very fast. They spawn frum

monster spawners They attak by jumping at there target. They are

very poisonous. When killed they can drop string or spider eye.

Busy as a bee.

ANIMAL SIMILES

Write the animal name that completes the simile.

A **simile** makes a comparison using *like* or *as*.

| mule | fox | bird | bunny | dog | bat | cat | horse |

1. free as a _____

2. blind as a _____

3. sick as a _____

4. hungry as a _____

5. stubborn as a _____

6. quick as a _____

7. curious as a _____

8. sly as a _____

MINECRAFT METAPHORS

Don't be a chicken!

Draw a line from the bolded metaphor to its meaning.

A **metaphor** describes something by comparing it to something else.

1. Steve was **a volcano ready to explode.**

2. Nitwit is **a funny duck.**

3. Zombie ran **lightning fast.**

4. Iron golem is **a giant.**

5. Bird is **music to Steve's ears.**

A. very quickly

B. really tall

C. really angry

D. sounds lovely

E. silly

IDIOMS

Circle the best meaning of the bolded idioms.

An **idiom** is a saying that has a different meaning from its literal meaning.

1. Steve mined **until the cows came home.**

A. He kept mining until the cows were in the pen.

B. He kept mining for a long time.

2. Alex found a diamond in the mine that **knocked her socks off.**

A. The diamond was better than Alex expected.

B. The diamond made Alex's sock fall off.

3. Steve wasn't afraid of dog because he **knew its bark was worse than its bite.**

A. The dog liked to bark a lot.

B. The dog was loud, but not dangerous.

4. When Alex met the baby mooshroom, she thought **the apple doesn't fall far from the tree.**

A. Alex thought the baby mooshroom looked just like its parent.

B. Alex thought the baby mooshroom was hungry and would like to eat an apple.

5. When Steve saw Creeper explode, he was **waiting for the other shoe to drop.**

A. Creeper's explosion caused Steve's shoes to fly up in the air.

B. Steve was waiting for something else to go wrong.

6. Alex and Steve were **laughing their heads off.**

A. They laughed so hard their block heads came off.

B. They laughed hard.

MORE IDIOMS

Circle the best meaning of the bolded idioms.

1. Alex was **over the moon** about her mobs.

A. Alex loved her mobs.
B. Alex went into space.

2. The villager gave witch **the cold shoulder.**

A. The villager ignored witch.
B. The villager hugged witch.

3. When Alex rode pig, **it was all ears.**

A. Pig had very large ears.
B. Pig listened to Alex.

4. The potion cost Wither an **arm and a leg.**

A. Wither lost its arms and legs when it drank the potion.
B. The potion cost Wither a lot.

5. Steve **drew a blank** during his math test.

A. Steve couldn't remember how to do the problem.
B. Steve drew a blank square on his math test.

6. Steve **called it a day** after exploring for hours.

A. Steve thought exploring should be called a day.
B. Steve quit exploring for the day.

WRITE A STORY

Use the characters, items, and setting pictured to write a story. Before writing, use the graphic organizer to plan your story.

Characters and Items

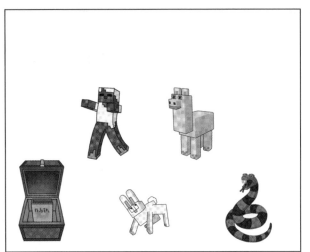

Setting

What is the problem to be solved?

Beginning or Introduction

Middle or Action

Ending or Solution

WRITE A STORY

_____

_____

_____

_____

_____

_____

_____

_____

_____

_____

WRITE AN OPINION

Do you think playing Minecraft is a good activity for kids? Write your opinion. Use the graphic organizer to plan your writing.

Your Opinion

Reason 1

Reason 2

Reason 3

Examples/evidence:

_____

_____

_____

_____

Examples/evidence:

_____

_____

_____

_____

Examples/evidence:

_____

_____

_____

_____

Your Conclusion

WRITE AN OPINION

_____

_____

_____

_____

_____

_____

_____

_____

_____

_____

_____

_____

I want to inform about how to tame a mob

WRITE TO INFORM

Write to inform a new player something about Minecraft. Use the graphic organizer to plan your informational writing.

Topic: _____

_____

Topic Sentence: _____

_____

_____

Fact 1	Fact 2	Fact 3

Concluding Sentence:

_____

_____

_____

WRITE TO INFORM

_____

_____

_____

_____

_____

_____

_____

_____

_____

_____

_____

_____

SEQUENCING EVENTS

Read how to craft a beacon. Write the steps in the correct order.

How to Craft a Beacon

Beacons are useful for creating light. They shine a light beam toward the sky. They also can melt snow and ice. In addition, they can give players status effects. To make a beacon you will need a crafting table, five glass blocks, three obsidian blocks, and a nether star. Place the three obsidian blocks along the bottom row of the crafting table. Place the nether star in the center of the table. Fill the rest of the table with the glass blocks. Set the beacon on a pyramid to activate it.

Steps to Crafting a Beacon

1. Get _____

2. Place _____

3. Place _____

4. Place _____

5. Set _____

LOGICAL THINKING

Read the clues to craft a Minecraft cake. Draw the ingredients on the crafting board.

Recipe for Cake

3 wheat

1 egg

2 sugar

3 milk

To make a cake you will need a 3 x 3 crafting board.

➡ Place the egg in the center.

➡ Place all the wheat on the same row.

➡ Place all the milk on the same row.

➡ Place the milk above the egg.

➡ Place the sugar.

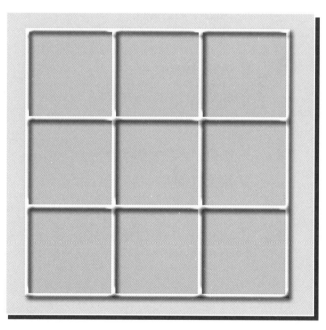

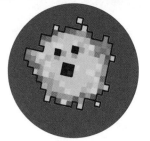

CAUSE AND EFFECT

Draw a line to match the cause with the effect.

Cause is the why something happens.

Effect is what happens.

1. If you press "use" on a donkey,

2. If a player finds a bat hanging upside-down,

3. If you have a monster spawner,

4. If a player eats a pufferfish,

5. If you kill a chicken,

A. the player will die.

B. it drops a feather.

C. it will screech and fly away.

D. a chest is added so it can carry things.

E. you can spawn mobs.

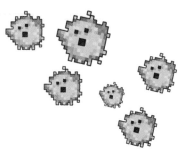

CAUSE AND EFFECT

Complete the missing parts of the chart to show cause and effect.

Cause	Effect
1. If you want to get metal from a block,	
2.	right click on a villager.
3. Because ocelots are passive, shy mobs,	
4.	you will need a saddle.
5. If you have a cooked rabbit, a carrot, a baked potato, a mushroom, and a bowl,	
6.	a skeleton will shoot arrows.

COMPARE AND CONTRAST

Compare and contrast two different villagers.

Compare means to tell how two or more things are alike.

Contrast means to tell how two or more things are different.

Villager 1   Villager 2

Color of clothing: _____   Color of clothing: _____

Job: _____   Job: _____

Where it lives: _____   Where it lives: _____

Passive or hostile? (circle one)   Passive or hostile? (circle one)

How are the villagers alike?

How are the villagers different?

ROUNDING NUMBERS

Round the numbers to the nearest 10.

We don't do a lot of rounding in Minecraft.

Rounding Rules

If the ones digit is less than 5, round the number **down** to the nearest 10.

If the ones digit is 5 or more, round the number **up** to the nearest 10.

1. 57 → _____

2. 65 → _____

3. 33 → _____

4. 17 → _____

5. 94 → _____

6. 23 → _____

7. 83 → _____

8. 15 → _____

9. 99 → _____

10. 6 → _____

11. 71 → _____

12. 52 → _____

13. 68 → _____

14. 25 → _____

15. 39 → _____

16. 42 → _____

17. 13 → _____

18. 70 → _____

NUMBERS TO 9999

Use place value to write the missing numbers in the blocks.

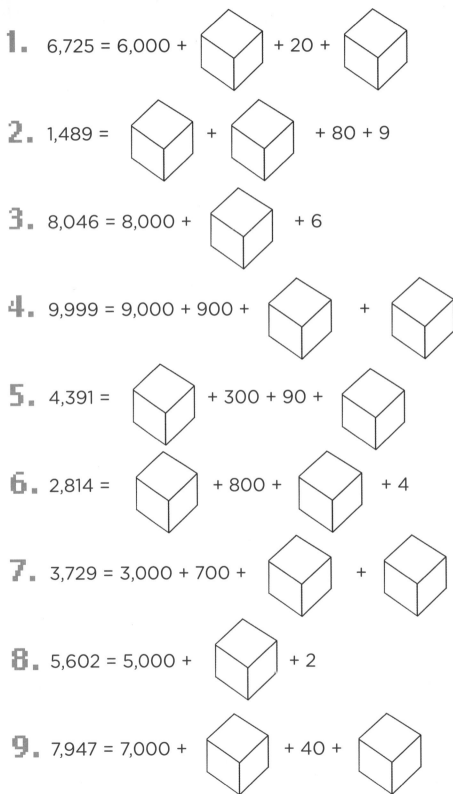

1. 6,725 = 6,000 + [ ] + 20 + [ ]

2. 1,489 = [ ] + [ ] + 80 + 9

3. 8,046 = 8,000 + [ ] + 6

4. 9,999 = 9,000 + 900 + [ ] + [ ]

5. 4,391 = [ ] + 300 + 90 + [ ]

6. 2,814 = [ ] + 800 + [ ] + 4

7. 3,729 = 3,000 + 700 + [ ] + [ ]

8. 5,602 = 5,000 + [ ] + 2

9. 7,947 = 7,000 + [ ] + 40 + [ ]

COMPARING NUMBERS TO 9999

Use <, >, or = to compare the numbers.

1. 3,466 ☐ 3,456

2. 7,817 ☐ 7,871

3. 4,543 ☐ 5,543

4. 2,727 ☐ 2,772

5. 7,089 ☐ 7,809

6. 8,369 ☐ 8,371

7. 4,004 ☐ 3,899

8. 6,009 ☐ 6,010

9. 9,917 ☐ 9,917

10. 1,008 ☐ 998

11. 2,801 ☐ 2,108

12. 4,732 ☐ 4,702

ADDITION

Solve the problems. Complete the puzzle.

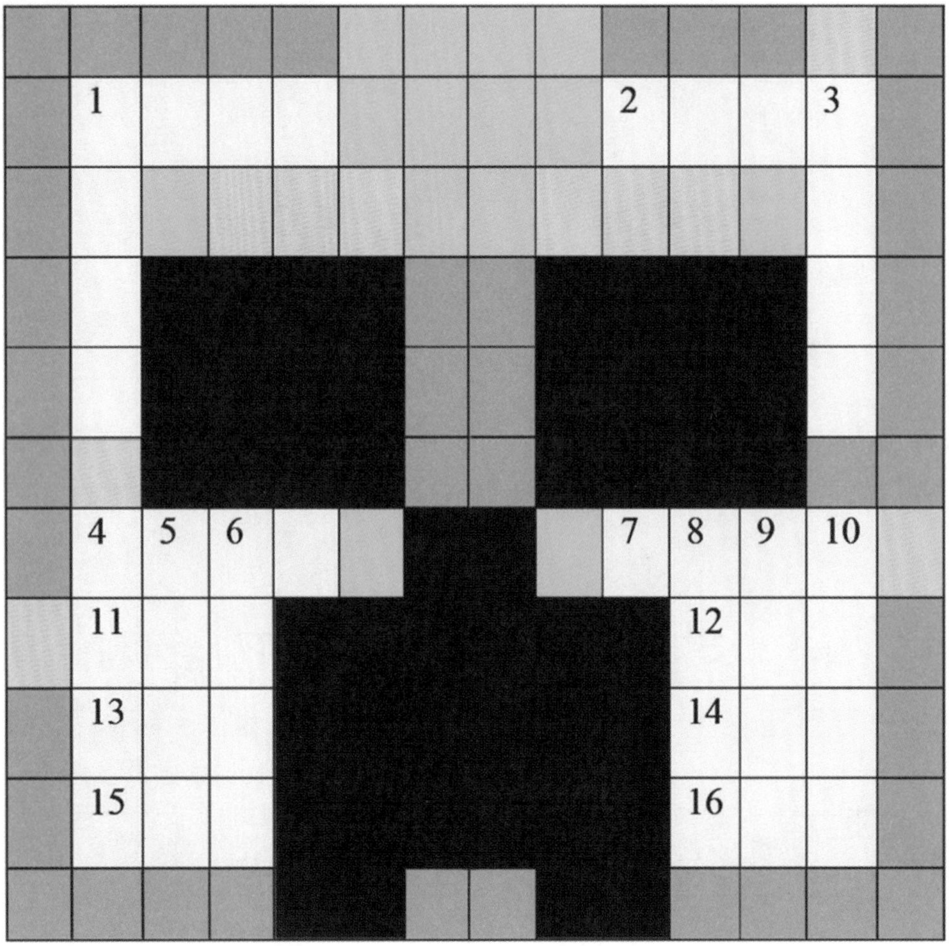

ACROSS

1 2,753 + 697

2 1,472 + 1,509

4 5,931 + 3,300

7 1,999 + 2,532

11 311 + 107

12 254 + 348

13 87 + 118

14 465 + 273

15 137 + 326

16 309 + 204

DOWN

1 1,340 + 1,936

3 1,080 + 302

4 7,816 + 1,608

5 1,497 + 609

6 1,319 + 2,534

8 2,798 + 2,877

9 3,000 + 31

10 814 + 469

ADDITION

Solve each problem. Use the answers to solve the riddle.

1. 631
   + 227

2. 525
   + 132

3. 733
   + 126

R   T   H

4. 171
   + 268

5. 142
   + 351

6. 483
   + 310

F   O   S

7. 253
   + 373

8. 338
   + 541

9. 654
   + 215

L   E   I

Q: What is the last thing that Steve takes off before going to bed?
COPY THE LETTERS FROM THE ANSWERS ABOVE TO FIND OUT.

859 869 793   439 879 879 657   493 439 439

657 859 879   439 626 493 493 858

SUBTRACTION

Solve the problems. Complete the puzzle.

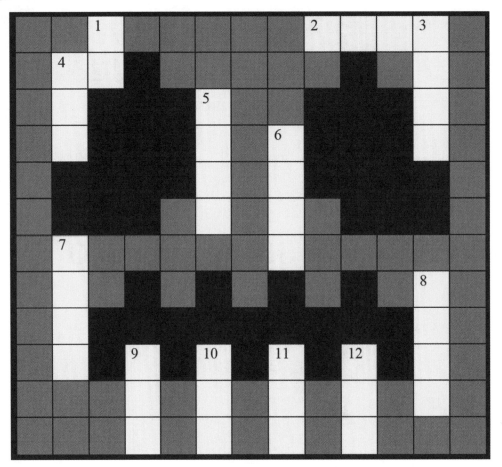

ACROSS

2 7,304 – 4992

4 4,742 – 4,715

DOWN

1 2,340 – 2,293

3 5,107 – 2,303

4 8,001 – 7,766

5 7,719 – 3,359

6 6,847 – 1640

7 9,843 – 5,982

8 6,874 – 831

9 7,100 – 6794

10 611 – 426

11 4,604 – 3,663

12 3,999 – 3,764

SUBTRACTION

Solve each problem. Use the answers to solve the riddle.

C – O – W

1. 426
  – 125

2. 325
  – 172

3. 513
  – 282

D

L

H

4. 671
  – 168

5. 346
  – 201

6. 483
  – 117

Y

O

S

7. 853
  – 326

8. 738
  – 544

9. 564
  – 215

U

E

B

Q: How do you spell cow using fourteen letters?
COPY THE LETTERS FROM THE ANSWERS ABOVE TO FIND OUT.

366 194 194   145   231

301 145 527 349 153 194   503 145 527

NUMBER PUZZLES

Complete the number puzzles using the numbers 1, 2, 3, 4, 5, and 6, so that each line (across and up and down) equals the number in the block.

1.

2
1

11

2.

3

12

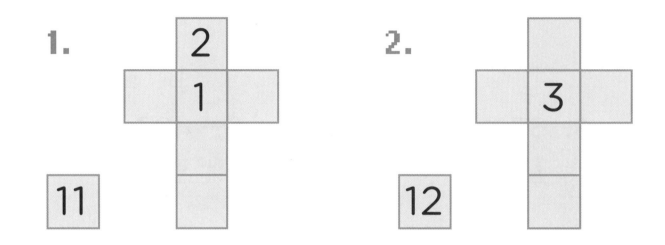

3.

5

13

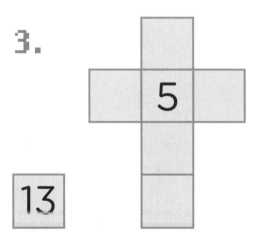

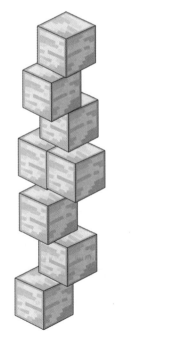

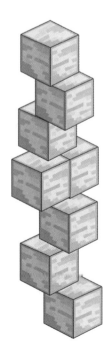

PROBLEM SOLVING IN THE ARCTIC

Read and solve each problem. Use the box to show how you solved the problem.

1. The Arctic Biome is home to 234 polar bears and 366 white rabbits. How many of these animals live in the Arctic Biome?

_____

2. There were 431 fish in the ocean surrounding the arctic biome. The polar bears ate 179 fish. How many fish were left?

_____

3. Steve spotted 327 adult polar bears. He said that there were 132 fewer baby polar bears than adult polar bears. How many baby polar bears did he see?

_____

4. Steve walked many steps across the frozen tundra of the Arctic Biome. He walked 523 steps the first day and 488 steps the second day. How many steps did he walk all together?

_____

SUMS AND PRODUCTS

Add the numbers to get the sum. Multiply the numbers to get the product. The first one is done for you.

1.

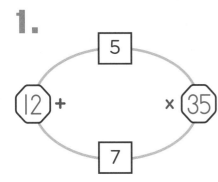

5

(12) + × (35)

7

2.

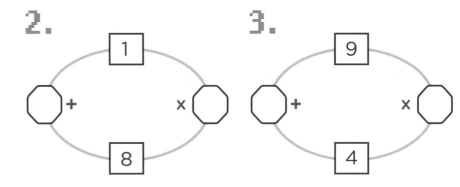

1

◯ + × ◯

8

3.

9

◯ + × ◯

4

4.

2

◯ + × ◯

5

5.

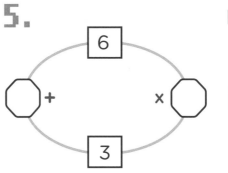

6

◯ + × ◯

3

6.

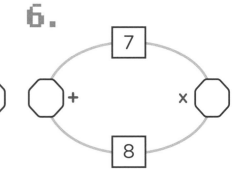

7

◯ + × ◯

8

7.

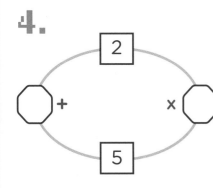

5

◯ + × ◯

9

8.

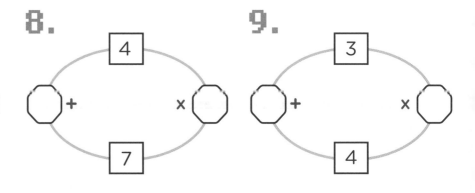

4

◯ + × ◯

7

9.

3

◯ + × ◯

4

MULTIPLICATION FACTS

Multiply the numbers by the center number. The first one is done for you.

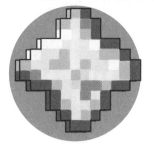

1.

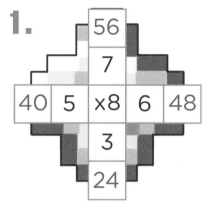

	56	
	7	
40 5	x8	6 48
	3	
	24	

2.

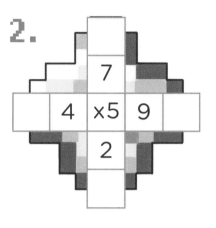

	7	
4	x5	9
	2	

3.

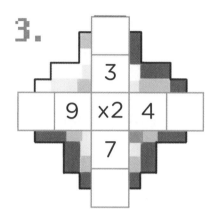

	3	
9	x2	4
	7	

4.

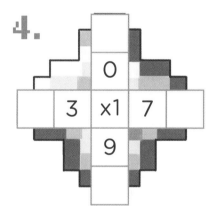

	0	
3	x1	7
	9	

5.

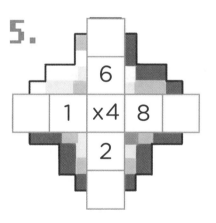

	6	
1	x4	8
	2	

6.

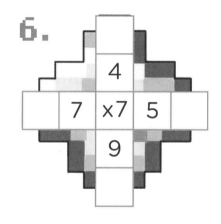

	4	
7	x7	5
	9	

7.

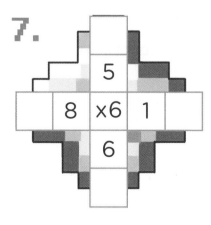

	5	
8	x6	1
	6	

8.

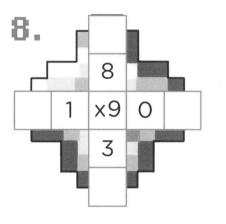

	8	
1	x9	0
	3	

9.

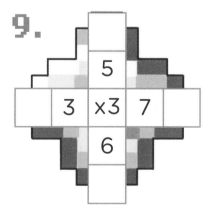

	5	
3	x3	7
	6	

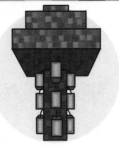

FACTORS

Draw a line to match the factor pairs. Cross out any numbers that are not factors. The first one is done for you.

Factors are the numbers that can be multiplied together to get a product.

The factors of 4 are 1, 2, and 4.   1 x 4 = 4   2 x 2 = 4

1. Factors of 20

1   10   4   ~~6~~

5   ~~3~~   2   20

2. Factors of 12

6   ~~7~~   12   3

1   4   2   ~~8~~

3. Factors of 24

24   6   3   2

8   12   4   1

4. Factors of 36

9   6   2   12   1

36   6   3   4   18

5. Factors of 42

7   8   42   3   2

21   9   6   1   14

6. Factors of 25

9   1   7   5

9   5   2   25

7. Factors of 27

27   7   4   9

2   3   1   6

8. Factors of 35

5   3   15   1

35   4   10   7

9. Factors of 48

6   3   48   12   2

24   4   8   1   16

FACTORS

Write the factor pairs on chicken's eggs.

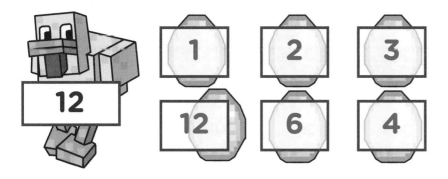

12 | 1 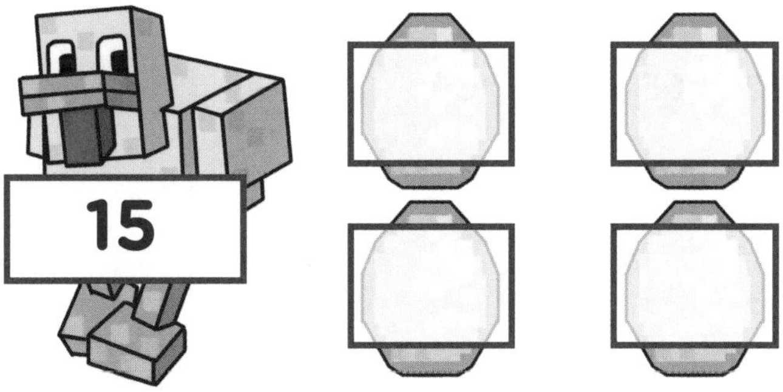 | 2 | 3 | 12 | 6 | 4

1.  15

2. 18

3. 24

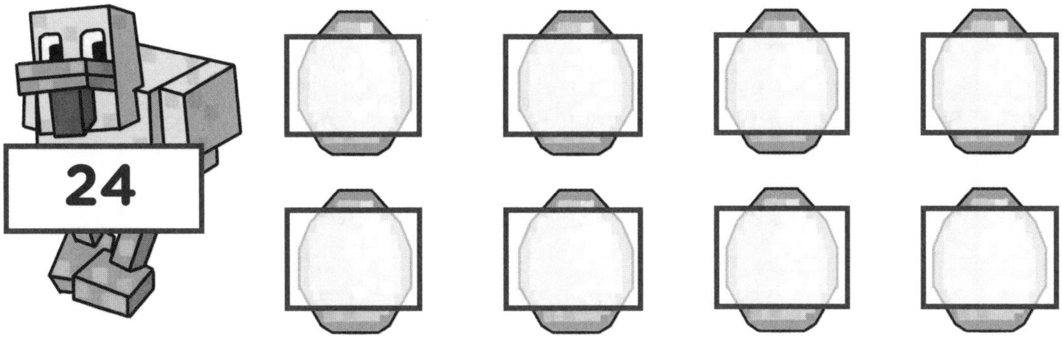

MULTIPLES

Color the multiples to help Zombie find his way safely around the lava

1. multiples of 3

START →

3	6	13	4	7	9	43	31	6	8
1	9	15	2	21	5	20	22	10	98
17	53	19	18	35	24	29	40	2	11
46	83	16	26	13	23	27	28	71	62
89	44	95	47	52	65	38	30	70	57
20	78	55	88	14	67	86	33	51	49
59	74	14	42	93	73	77	36	39	68
12	52	22	61	50	25	80	23	37	42

END

2. multiples of 4

START →

4	8	7	16	14	13	6	19	9	21
30	5	12	2	20	19	27	22	1	42
64	3	10	15	24	35	33	51	17	32
58	14	29	70	28	34	78	53	49	45
90	37	47	32	6	73	86	94	99	50
83	74	43	69	36	11	57	2	25	63
81	39	12	77	51	40	44	48	18	17
61	34	95	76	22	55	66	82	52	56

END

MORE MULTIPLES

Color the multiples to help Zombie find his way safely around the lava.

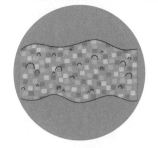

1. multiples of 5

START →

5	12	17	21	2	6	19	27	11	8
10	15	24	22	3	9	18	1	7	16
14	13	20	27	30	35	28	33	29	31
72	61	59	25	53	46	40	47	39	37
88	84	66	78	91	94	45	56	58	62
97	92	83	79	69	89	74	50	99	78
28	36	49	52	80	19	83	55	73	81
77	54	48	37	61	93	76	60	65	70

END

2. multiples of 9

START →

9	18	32	11	31	7	49	8	18	21
1	2	27	3	6	67	19	20	47	36
14	39	40	36	45	10	4	9	5	12
38	29	25	17	54	44	76	13	55	53
50	89	82	15	60	63	98	73	69	70
62	12	28	97	85	79	72	81	37	64
49	21	46	95	23	77	86	66	90	83
84	13	67	30	52	88	80	57	42	99

END

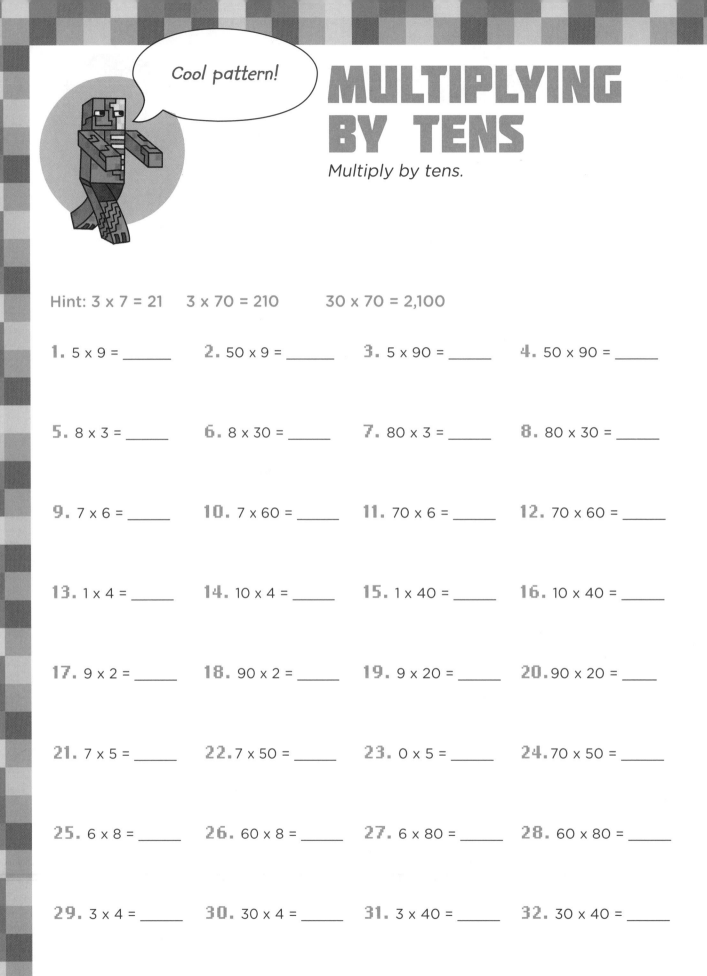

Cool pattern!

MULTIPLYING BY TENS

Multiply by tens.

Hint: 3 x 7 = 21   3 x 70 = 210   30 x 70 = 2,100

1. 5 x 9 = _____

2. 50 x 9 = _____

3. 5 x 90 = _____

4. 50 x 90 = _____

5. 8 x 3 = _____

6. 8 x 30 = _____

7. 80 x 3 = _____

8. 80 x 30 = _____

9. 7 x 6 = _____

10. 7 x 60 = _____

11. 70 x 6 = _____

12. 70 x 60 = _____

13. 1 x 4 = _____

14. 10 x 4 = _____

15. 1 x 40 = _____

16. 10 x 40 = _____

17. 9 x 2 = _____

18. 90 x 2 = _____

19. 9 x 20 = _____

20. 90 x 20 = _____

21. 7 x 5 = _____

22. 7 x 50 = _____

23. 0 x 5 = _____

24. 70 x 50 = _____

25. 6 x 8 = _____

26. 60 x 8 = _____

27. 6 x 80 = _____

28. 60 x 80 = _____

29. 3 x 4 = _____

30. 30 x 4 = _____

31. 3 x 40 = _____

32. 30 x 40 = _____

MULTIPLYING BY 10, 100, 1,000

Multiply to complete the chart.

I feel like a genius with multiplying by 10, 100, and 1,000.

Multiply to complete the chart.

	x10	x100	x1,000
1. 24			
2. 15			
3. 27			
4. 36			
5. 42			
6. 61			
7. 58			
8. 73			
9. 86			
10. 90			

MULTIPLYING

Find the product of each problem. Then use the key to color.

less than 1,000	1,000 – 1,999	2,000 – 2,999	3,000 – 3,999	4,000 and over

				23 x45			
			56 x16	33 x21	29 x19		
			49 x17	59 x16	15 x47		
	65 x61		64 x29	22 x44	37 x38		
		82 x40	11 x36	85 x62	18 x42		72 x54
			98 x45	77 x69	61 x88	58 x58	
				59 x68			
				64 x93		44 x52	
		35 x58		53 x79	49 x47		
			59 x42	99 x99			
				83 x78			
		95 x38		64 x87		86 x45	
78 x51	86 x95		24 x89	73 x92	33 x65		43 x77
	73 x54	70 x85	90 x44	35 x60	66 x89	36 x85	53 x48

MULTIPLYING

Solve each problem. Use the answers to solve the riddle.

1. 23
   x 27

2. 65
   x 32

3. 43
   x 46

4. 30
   x 25

A

T

N

H

5. 71
   x 68

6. 42
   x 51

7. 23
   x 31

8. 13
   x 52

G

O

W

D

9. 53
   x 33

10. 34
    x 42

11. 54
    x 15

12. 33
    x 44

B

I

Y

E

Q: Why didn't skeleton go to the party?

COPY THE LETTERS FROM THE ANSWERS ABOVE TO FIND OUT.

750   1,452   750   621   676   1,978   2,142   1,749   2,142   676   810

2,080   2,142   4,828   2,142   713   1,428   2,080   750

315

DIVISION FACTS

Solve the problems. Use the key to color the orb.

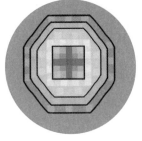

1	2	3	4	5,6	6,7	8,9

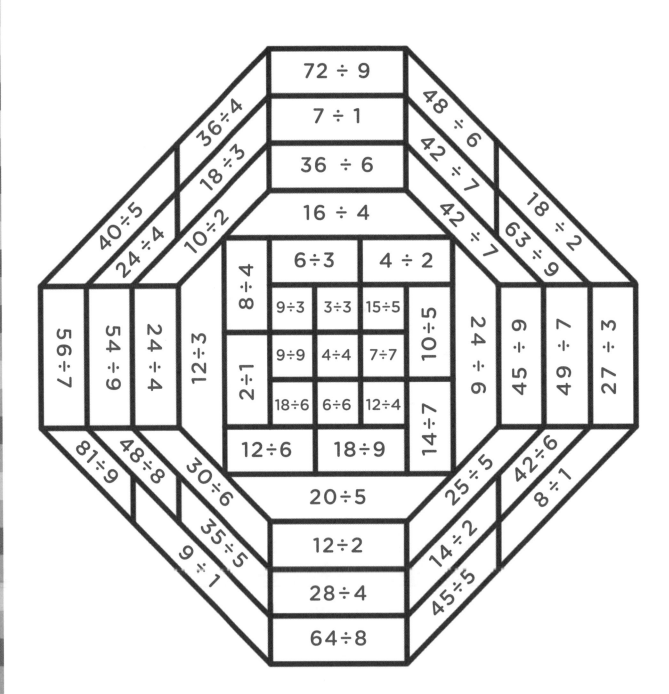

72 ÷ 9

7 ÷ 1

36 ÷ 6

16 ÷ 4

36÷4

18 ÷ 3

40÷5

24 ÷ 4

10÷2

48 ÷ 6

42 ÷ 7

42 ÷ 7

18 ÷ 2

63 ÷ 9

6÷3

4 ÷ 2

8 ÷ 4

9÷3

3÷3

15÷5

10÷5

9÷9

4÷4

7÷7

2÷1

18÷6

6÷6

12÷4

14÷7

12÷6

18÷9

56÷7

54÷9

24 ÷ 4

12÷3

24 ÷ 6

45 ÷ 9

49 ÷ 7

27 ÷ 3

81÷9

48÷8

30÷6

20÷5

25 ÷ 5

42÷6

8 ÷ 1

35÷5

12÷2

14 ÷ 2

9 ÷ 1

28 ÷ 4

45÷5

64÷8

316

DIVISION FACTS

Complete the missing numbers in the division equations.
The first one is done for you.

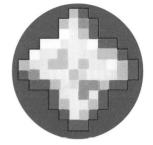

1.

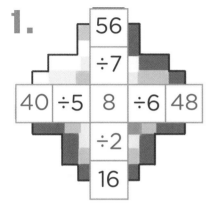

56
÷7
40 ÷5 8 ÷6 48
÷2
16

2.

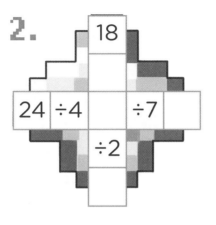

18
24 ÷4 ÷7
÷2

3.

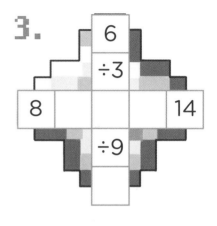

6
÷3
8 14
÷9

4.

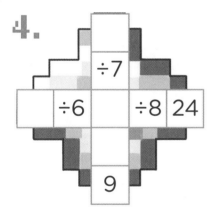

÷7
÷6 ÷8 24
9

5.

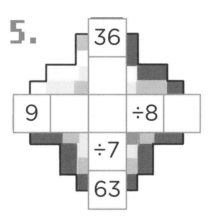

36
9 ÷8
÷7
63

6.

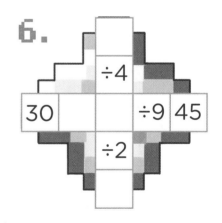

÷4
30 ÷9 45
÷2

7.

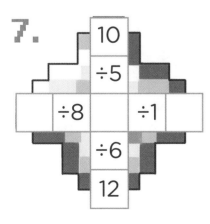

10
÷5
÷8 ÷1
÷6
12

8.

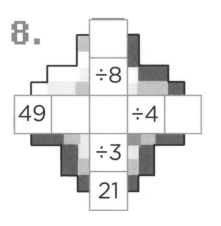

÷8
49 ÷4
÷3
21

9.

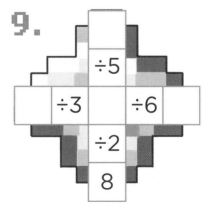

÷5
÷3 ÷6
÷2
8

317

DIVISION WITH REMAINDERS

Solve each problem. Use the answers to solve the riddle.

1. 3)29

2. 5)36

3. 7)48

4. 9)82

5. 8)20

A   C   E   L   O

6. 4)19

7. 6)57

8. 3)16

9. 2)17

10. 5)27

V   U   S   P   N

11. 8)46

12. 5)22

13. 7)29

14. 9)35

15. 3)20

T   G   H   I   D

Q: Why did pig spread a blanket on the ground?

COPY THE LETTERS FROM THE ANSWERS ABOVE TO FIND OUT.

5R1   2R4   3R8   5R6   7R1   2R4   9R3   9R1   6R2

4R1   9R2   4R3   6R6   9R2   8R1   3R8   4R2   5R2   3R8   7R1

DIVISION WITH REMAINDERS

Draw a line from the problem on Steve's minecart to the block that shows the answer.

1.  58÷9

A.  8R4

2.  60÷7

B.  5R6

3.  37÷5

C.  6R4

4. 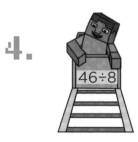 46÷8

D.  7R2

5.  27÷6

E.  4R3

MOB'S MATH

Read and solve each problem. Use the box to show how you solved the problem.

1. 27 zombies spawned at the edge of the village. Each zombie spawned 3 baby zombies. How many zombies (adult and baby zombies) were there?

_____

2. There were 46 zombies and 9 monster spawners that the zombies shared equally. How many zombies used each of the monster spawners?

_____

3. Steve saw 19 creepers hiding behind the house and three times as many hiding in the forest. How many creepers did Steve see?

_____

4. There were 6 sand pits in the desert. 15 husks were trapped in each pit. How many husks were trapped in the sand pits?

_____

MOB'S MATH

Read and solve each problem. Use the box to show how you solved the problem.

1. 42 iron golems lived in the village. They each gave 3 flowers to the villagers. How many flowers were given away?

_____

2. The librarian stacked lots of books. He had 77 books and 6 shelves. How many books were on each shelf?

_____

3. Mooshrooms were spawning everywhere. There were 63 mooshrooms spawned in one week. How many mooshrooms were spawned each day?

_____

4. Nitwit was having trouble figuring out how many apples he has on his apple trees. He has 232 trees and 10 apples on each tree. How many apples does he have?

_____

321

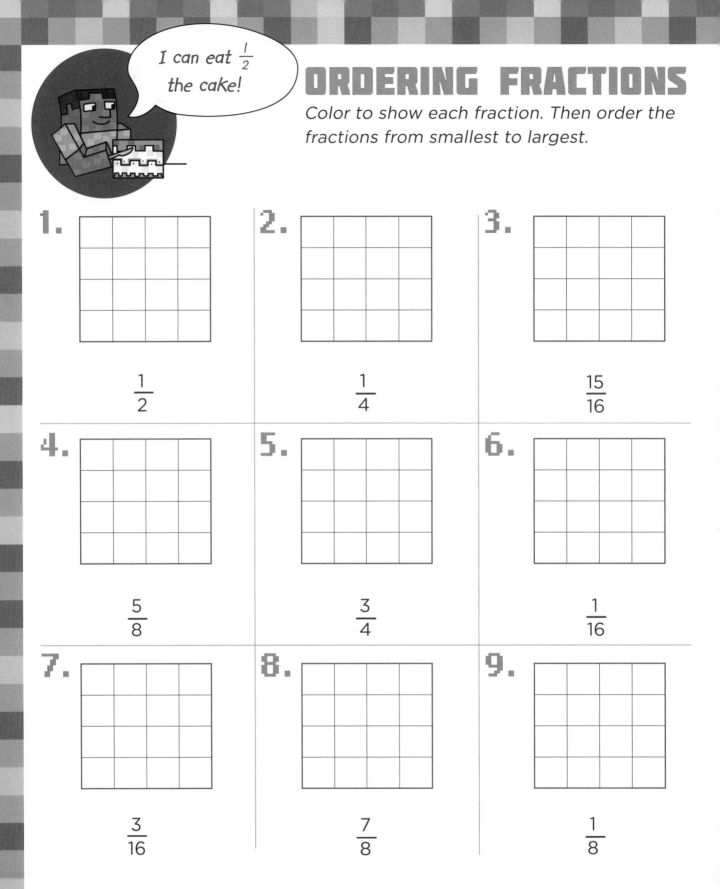

I can eat $\frac{1}{2}$ the cake!

ORDERING FRACTIONS

Color to show each fraction. Then order the fractions from smallest to largest.

1.

$\frac{1}{2}$

2.

$\frac{1}{4}$

3.

$\frac{15}{16}$

4.

$\frac{5}{8}$

5.

$\frac{3}{4}$

6.

$\frac{1}{16}$

7.

$\frac{3}{16}$

8.

$\frac{7}{8}$

9.

$\frac{1}{8}$

Write the fractions from smallest to largest.

_____ _____ _____ _____ _____ _____ _____ _____ _____

EQUIVALENT FRACTIONS

Color to show each fraction. Draw a line to match the equivalent fractions.

These towers are equivalent.

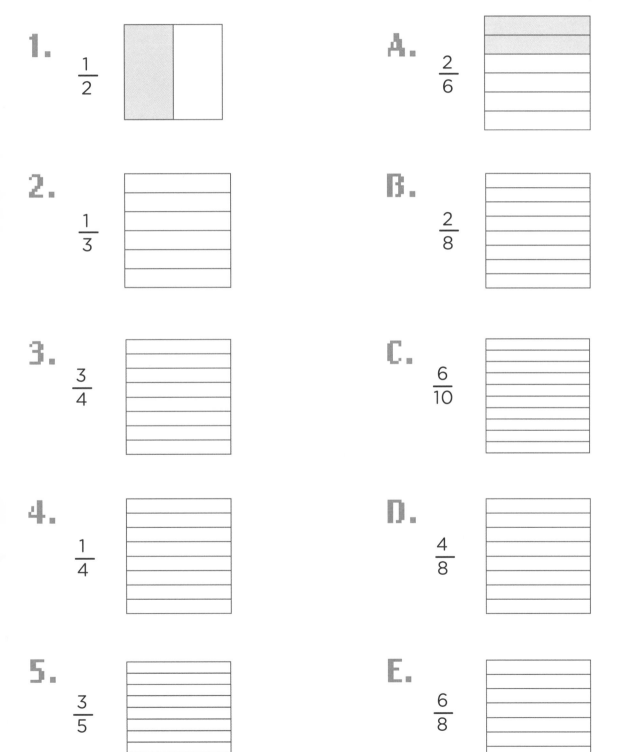

1. $\frac{1}{2}$

2. $\frac{1}{3}$

3. $\frac{3}{4}$

4. $\frac{1}{4}$

5. $\frac{3}{5}$

A. $\frac{2}{6}$

B. $\frac{2}{8}$

C. $\frac{6}{10}$

D. $\frac{4}{8}$

E. $\frac{6}{8}$

ADDING FRACTIONS

Write each fraction, then add.

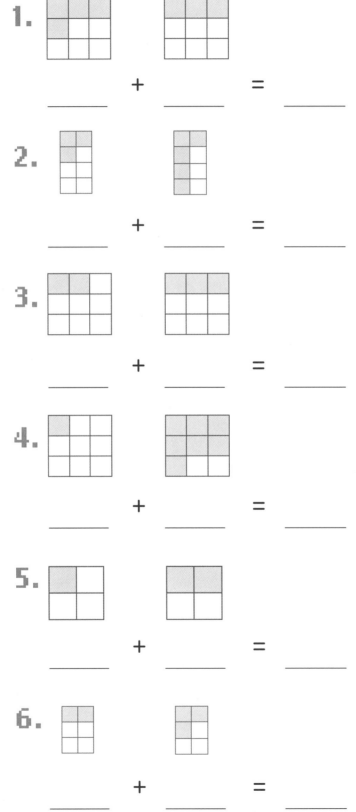

1. _____ + _____ = _____

2. _____ + _____ = _____

3. _____ + _____ = _____

4. _____ + _____ = _____

5. _____ + _____ = _____

6. _____ + _____ = _____

SUBTRACTING FRACTIONS

Subtract the fractions. Color to show the first fraction. Then cross out the second fraction. Write the fraction that remains.

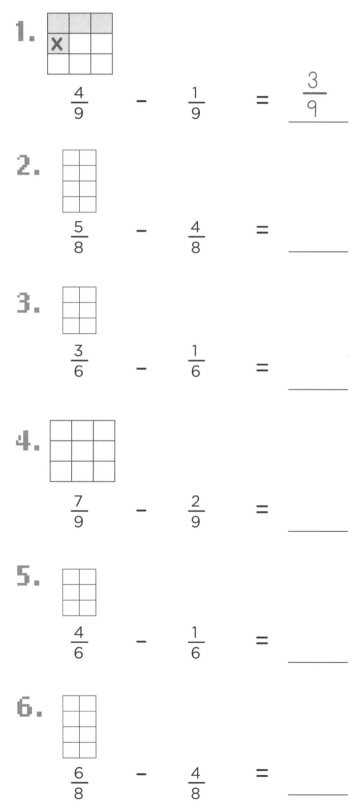

1. $\dfrac{4}{9}$ − $\dfrac{1}{9}$ = $\dfrac{3}{9}$

2. $\dfrac{5}{8}$ − $\dfrac{4}{8}$ = _____

3. $\dfrac{3}{6}$ − $\dfrac{1}{6}$ = _____

4. $\dfrac{7}{9}$ − $\dfrac{2}{9}$ = _____

5. $\dfrac{4}{6}$ − $\dfrac{1}{6}$ = _____

6. $\dfrac{6}{8}$ − $\dfrac{4}{8}$ = _____

MULTIPLY FRACTIONS BY WHOLE NUMBERS

Multiply the fractions.

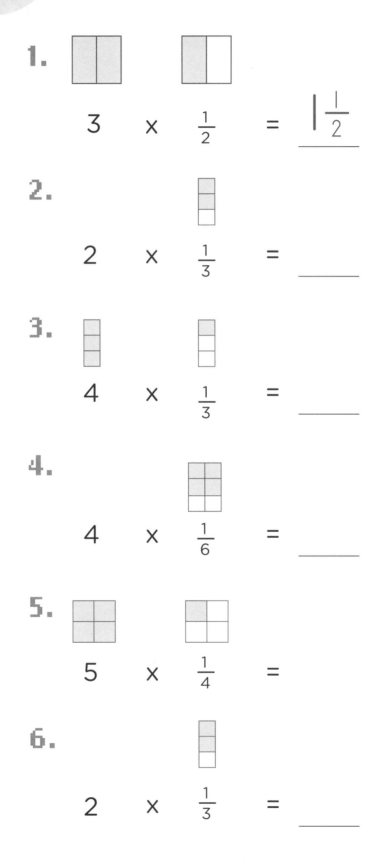

1. 3   x $\frac{1}{2}$ = $1\frac{1}{2}$

2. 2   x $\frac{1}{3}$ =   _____

3. 4   x $\frac{1}{3}$ =   _____

4. 4   x $\frac{1}{6}$ =   _____

5. 5   x $\frac{1}{4}$ =

6. 2   x $\frac{1}{3}$ =   _____

COOKING WITH WITCH

Read and solve each problem. Use the box to show how you solved the problem.

1. Witch needs $\frac{1}{2}$ cup sugar for the potion of swiftness. He wants to make 3 batches. How much sugar will he need all together?

_____

2. Witch needs $\frac{1}{5}$ cup of blaze powder for one batch of potion of strength and $\frac{3}{5}$ cup of blaze powder for another batch of potion of strength. How much blaze powder does he need all together? _____

3. Witch found $\frac{2}{3}$ of a glistening melon in the front yard and $\frac{1}{3}$ of a glistening melon in the back yard. How much of a glistening melon did he have all together?

_____

4. Witch had a cup of sugar. He needed $\frac{1}{4}$ of a cup to make a potion of swiftness. How much sugar did he have left over?

_____

DECIMALS

Write each fraction as a decimal.

Decimals are another way to show fractions or numbers less than one.

$\frac{7}{10} = .7$

$\frac{7}{100} = .07$

$\frac{17}{100} = .17$

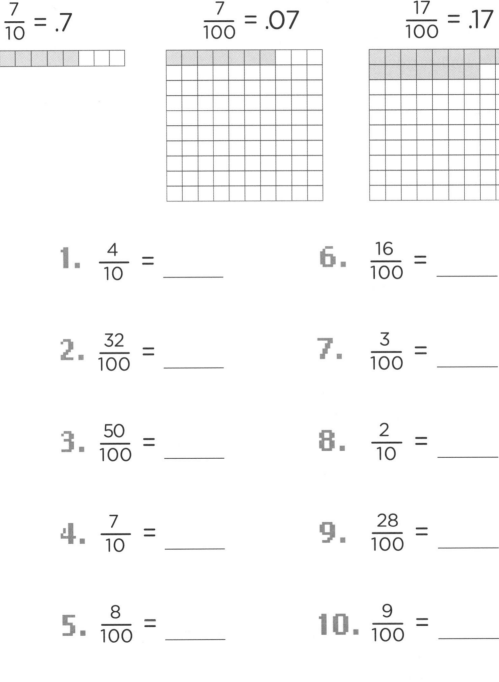

1. $\frac{4}{10}$ = _____

2. $\frac{32}{100}$ = _____

3. $\frac{50}{100}$ = _____

4. $\frac{7}{10}$ = _____

5. $\frac{8}{100}$ = _____

6. $\frac{16}{100}$ = _____

7. $\frac{3}{100}$ = _____

8. $\frac{2}{10}$ = _____

9. $\frac{28}{100}$ = _____

10. $\frac{9}{100}$ = _____

Which number is the smallest?

_____

Which number is the largest?

_____

DECIMALS

Write the fraction and the decimal of each shaded part.

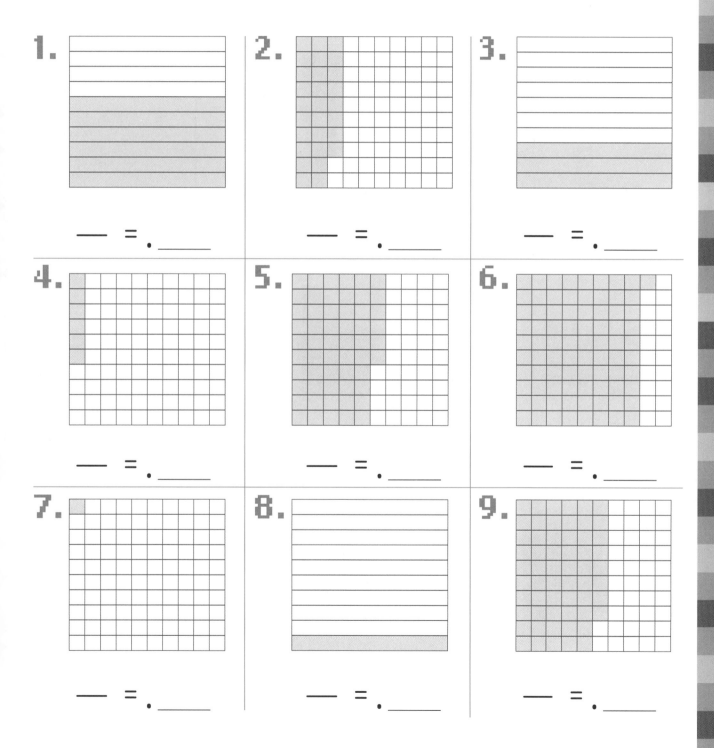

1. ____ ___ = . ____

2. ____ ___ = . ____

3. ____ ___ = . ____

4. ____ ___ = . ____

5. ____ ___ = . ____

6. ____ ___ = . ____

7. ____ ___ = . ____

8. ____ ___ = . ____

9. ____ ___ = . ____

STAIR PATTERNS

Look at the pyramid patterns. Complete the chart.
Draw the last stairs with 8 steps.

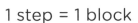

1 step = 1 block

2 steps = 3 blocks

3 steps = 6 blocks

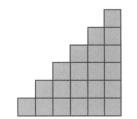

4 steps = _____ blocks

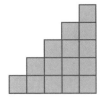

5 steps = _____ blocks

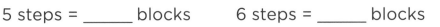

6 steps = _____ blocks

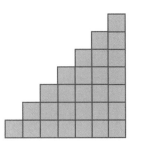

7 steps = _____ blocks

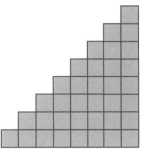

8 steps = _____ blocks

Steps	Number of blocks
1	1
2	3
3	6
4	
5	
6	
7	
8	

PYRAMID PATTERNS

Look at the pyramid patterns. Complete the chart.
Draw the fifth pyramid.

1.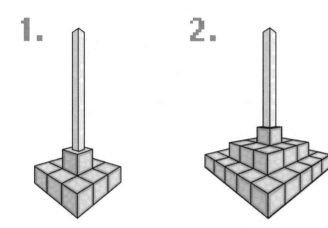

2.

3.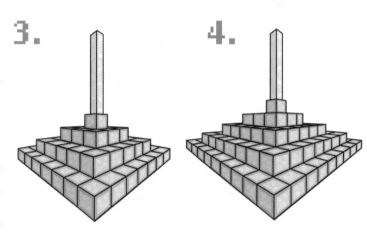

4.

Pyramid	Pyramid Base Size	Number of blocks
1	3 x 3 = 9	9
2	5 x 5 = 25	34
3	7 x 7 =	
4	9 x 9 =	
5		

5.

PERIMETER

Perimeter is the distance around a shape.

Look at the measurements around the farm.
Write the perimeter of each.

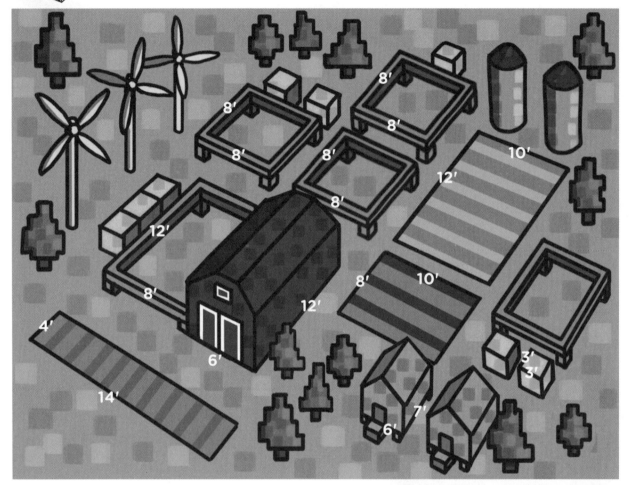

1. barn _____

2. one chicken house _____

3. pen beside the barn _____

4. corn crop _____

5. one of the pens behind the barn _____

6. lettuce crop _____

7. one bale of hay _____

8. green pepper crop _____

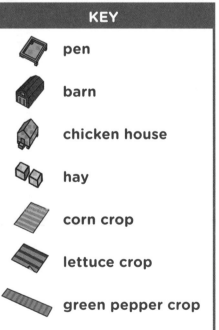

KEY
pen
barn
chicken house
hay
corn crop
lettuce crop
green pepper crop

332

AREA

Find the area of each square.

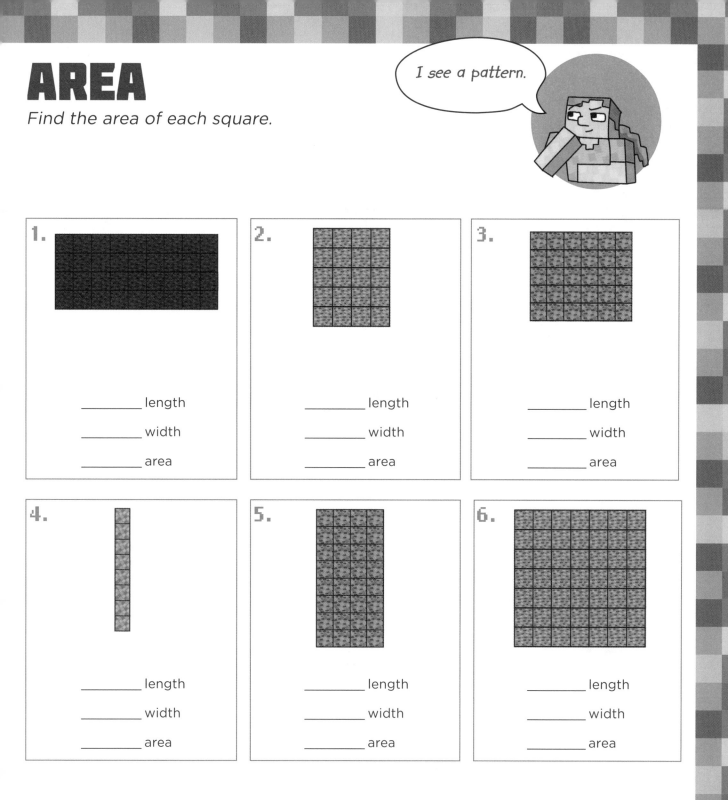

1.

_____ length

_____ width

_____ area

2.

_____ length

_____ width

_____ area

3.

_____ length

_____ width

_____ area

4.

_____ length

_____ width

_____ area

5.

_____ length

_____ width

_____ area

6.

_____ length

_____ width

_____ area

7. What pattern do you see in the numbers? This pattern is a formula for finding the area of a rectangle. _____

_____

_____

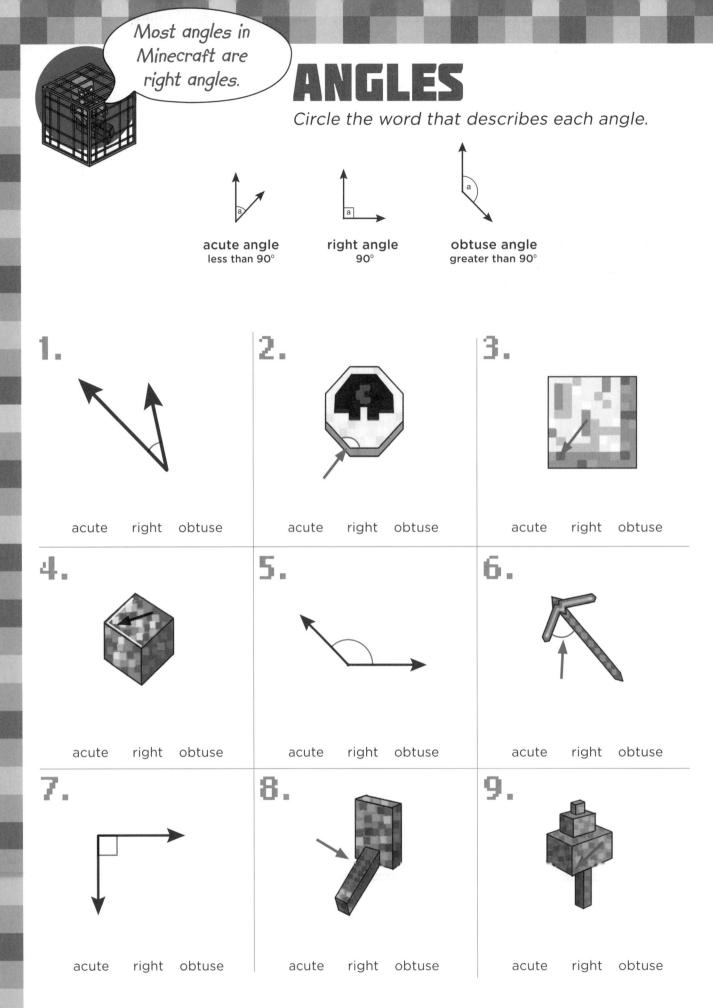

Most angles in Minecraft are right angles.

ANGLES

Circle the word that describes each angle.

acute angle
less than 90°

right angle
90°

obtuse angle
greater than 90°

1.

acute   right   obtuse

2.

acute   right   obtuse

3.

acute   right   obtuse

4.

acute   right   obtuse

5.

acute   right   obtuse

6.

acute   right   obtuse

7.

acute   right   obtuse

8.

acute   right   obtuse

9.

acute   right   obtuse

ANGLES

*Write **acute**, **obtuse**, or **right** to describe each angle.*

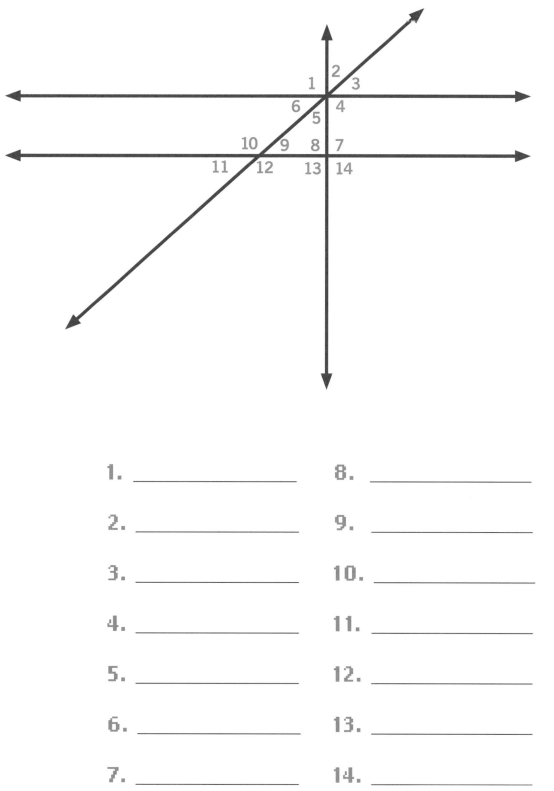

1. _____

2. _____

3. _____

4. _____

5. _____

6. _____

7. _____

8. _____

9. _____

10. _____

11. _____

12. _____

13. _____

14. _____

LINES

Lines are made up of points. Study the different types of lines in the chart. Answer the questions.

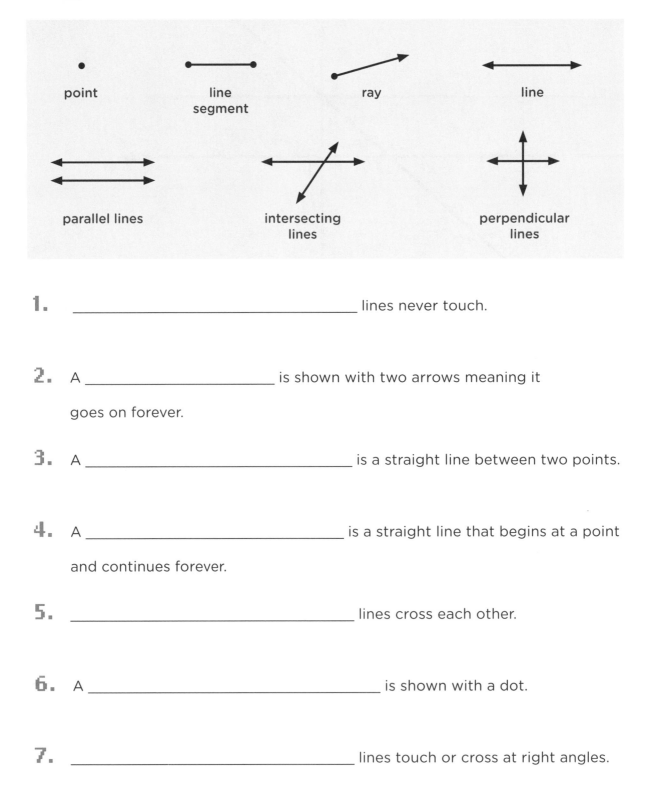

point	line segment	ray	line
parallel lines	intersecting lines	perpendicular lines	

1. _____ lines never touch.

2. A _____ is shown with two arrows meaning it goes on forever.

3. A _____ is a straight line between two points.

4. A _____ is a straight line that begins at a point and continues forever.

5. _____ lines cross each other.

6. A _____ is shown with a dot.

7. _____ lines touch or cross at right angles.

DRAWING WITH LINES

Follow the directions to create the line pictures.

1. Draw 10 rays shining from the sun.

2. Draw a track for Steve's minecart that includes 2 parallel line segments and 4 perpendicular line segments between the parallel line segments.

3. Draw another diamond sword that intersects with the sword pictured.

4. Connect the points (dots) to create snow golem.

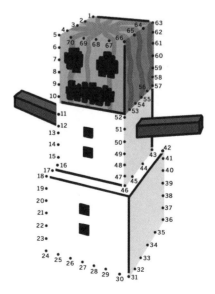

A square has two
sets of parallel lines.

LINES AND SHAPES

Follow the directions to create or mark the lines.
The first one is done for you.

1. Make the line segments into lines.

2. Color one set of parallel lines blue. Color the other set of parallel lines red.

3. Mark an X where the line segments intersect

4. Color the perpendicular lines green.

5. Color one set of parallel lines blue. Color the other set of parallel lines red.

RESPIRATORY SYSTEM

Read about the respiratory system.
Label the parts.

My respiratory system helps me blow the dandelion!

The respiratory system makes it possible for us to take in fresh air and get rid of stale air. Air enters the body through the **nose** and **mouth**. Then the air moves through the **larynx** to the **trachea**. From the trachea, the air enters the **lungs**. We have two lungs. Both lungs have small tubes called the **bronchi**. The bronchi fill up with air and expand the lungs. The **diaphragm** is a muscle under the lungs. It helps the lungs fill with air. It also helps to push the air out of the lungs.

diaphragm	trachea	larynx	lungs
mouth	nose	bronchi	

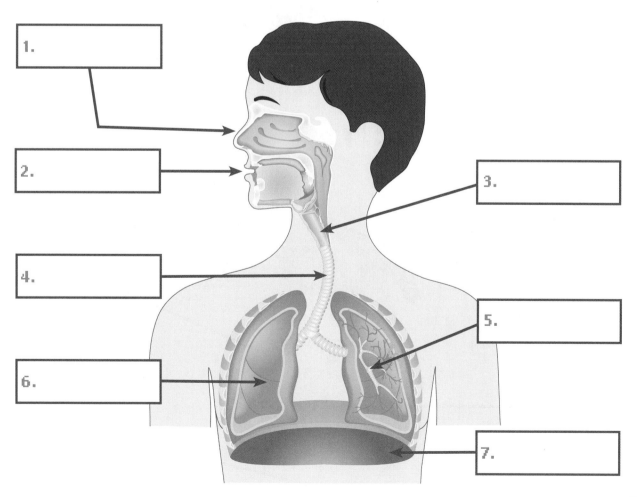

1.

2.

3.

4.

5.

6.

7.

DIGESTIVE SYSTEM

Let's see how my body uses this cake.

Read about the digestive system. Draw a line to trace the path that food travels through the body.

The digestive system changes food into energy. Food enters into the digestive system through the **mouth** where it is chewed. The food travels down the **esophagus** to the **stomach**. The stomach breaks down the food. Then the food enters the **small intestines**. The small intestines absorb the nutrients to make the body strong. The food then moves to the **large intestines**. The large intestines absorb water from the food. Food that is not used leaves the body through the **rectum**.

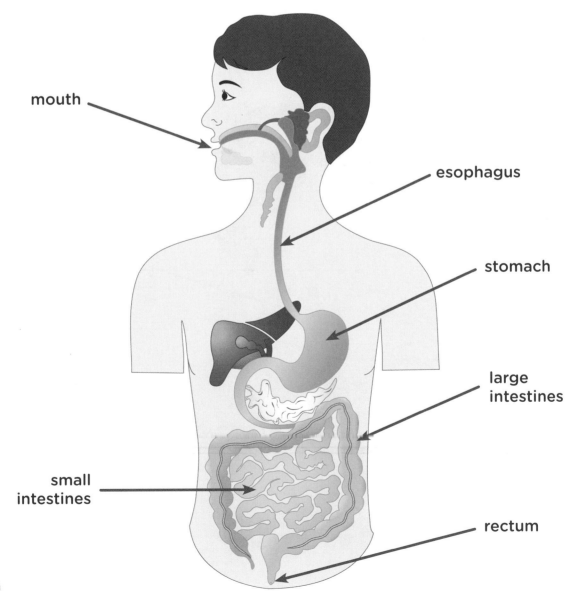

mouth

esophagus

stomach

large intestines

small intestines

rectum

CIRCULATORY SYSTEM

Read about the circulatory system. Color the veins blue and the arteries red. Draw arrows to show how the blood moves through the body. Label the heart.

♥ means health.

The circulatory system is the way the blood travels through the body. It is made up of muscles and organs. The heart is the most important muscle in our body. **Veins** carry blood toward the heart. **Arteries** carry the blood away from the heart. It takes the blood only a few seconds to travel through the whole body.

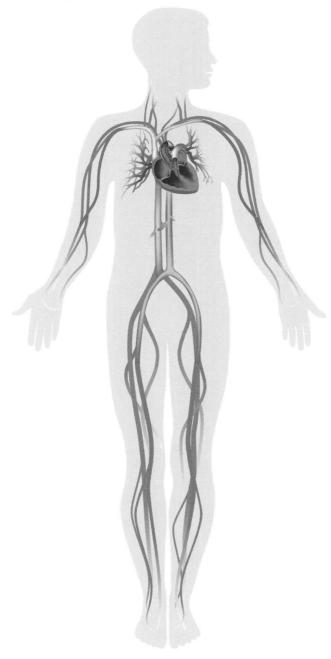

NERVOUS SYSTEM

Read about the nervous system. Label the parts.

The nervous system is made up of the **brain**, **spinal cord**, and **nerves**. The brain is in the skull. It sends commands down the spinal cord and through the nerves to the different parts of the body. The brain tells the muscles when and how to move. It controls the heart's beating and the lungs' breathing. The brain's job is to protect the body. Taking a deep breath is one way to calm the brain.

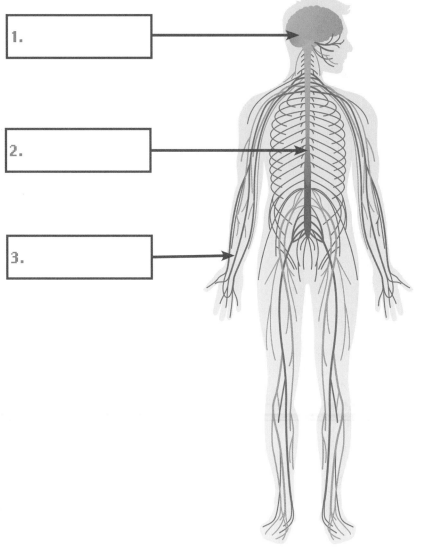

1.

2.

3.

SKELETAL SYSTEM

Read about the skeletal system. Circle the names of the bones in the puzzle.

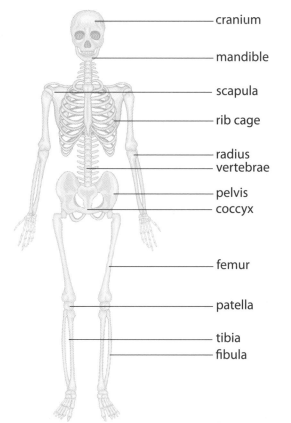

cranium

mandible

scapula

rib cage

radius
vertebrae

pelvis

coccyx

femur

patella

tibia
fibula

The skeletal system is made up of 106 bones. The bones give structure to the body. The bones protect the organs in the body.

```
V E R T E B R A E R D
P R L R X A P S N D T
D A W B I Y C N C N B
R J T B I A C R R Z J
I F I E P D A C T Y P
B T I U L N S O E B
C Y L B I L U A L C R
A A Y U U I A V M U D
G L M Q D L I D M D Y
E W X A J S A E Z R B
B D R R G D F T P J D
```

cranium

mandible

scapula

rib cage

radius

vertebrae

pelvis

coccyx

femur

patella

tibia

fibula

MUSCULAR SYSTEM

Read about the muscular system. Answer the question with a full sentence.

Muscles help the body to walk, stand, and sit. There are hundreds of muscles in the body. Our muscles need movement and healthy foods to grow.

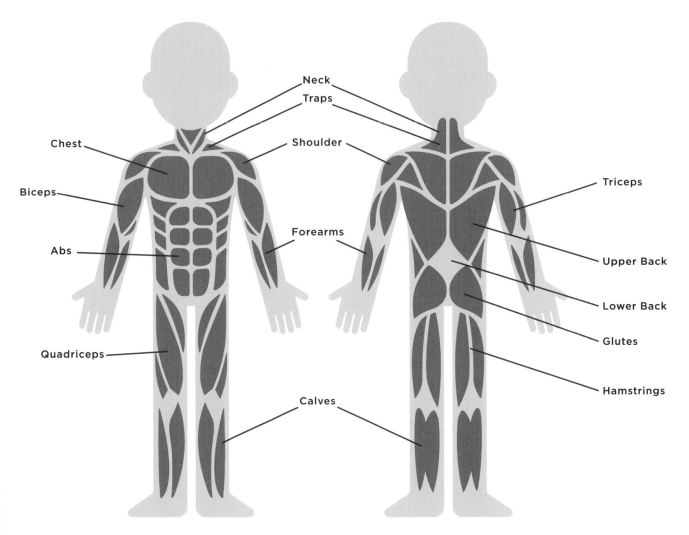

Neck
Traps
Chest
Shoulder
Biceps
Triceps
Forearms
Abs
Upper Back
Lower Back
Glutes
Quadriceps
Hamstrings
Calves

What is your favorite way to move your muscles?

_____

_____

_____

ECOSYSTEMS

Read about ecosystems. Draw arrows to show the transfer of energy through the ecosystem.

An ecosystem is an area where plants and animals interact with each other. Plants and animals also interact with the sun, soil, and water. In an ecosystem the sun provides energy to the plants. The plants use the energy from the sun to make their own food. Plants also get food from the soil. Some animals eat plants for energy. Other animals eat animals for energy. This transfer of energy in an ecosystem is called a food chain.

PREDATORS AND PREY

Read about animal predators and their prey. Draw an arrow pointing from each predator to its prey. Hint: Some animals may have more than one prey.

All animals need food to live. Animals get their food from plants or other animals. A **predator** is an animal that hunts other animals to eat. A **prey** is an animal that is hunted as food. Some animals are both predators and prey for other animals. For example, when a hawk eats a snake, the hawk is a predator and the snake is the prey. But when an ocelot eats a hawk, the ocelot is the predator and the hawk is its prey.

PREDATORS AND PREY

Read the sentences. Write which animal is the predator and which is the prey.

	Predator	Prey
1. An ocelot can be tamed with cod.		
2. The fish hid in the seaweed from the shark.		
3. The frog caught a fly with its long tongue.		
4. The bird watched over its eggs to keep the snake from eating them.		
5. The wolf stalked the rabbit.		
6. The worm inched across the grass before the bird ate it.		

ANSWER KEY

PAGE 255

1. Nitwit is a villager with no profession. 2. Fishing rods are tools used to catch fish. 3. The job of the Ender crystal is to heal the Ender Dragon. 4. The player built a lava pit and the zombie fell into it.

PAGE 256

1. D; 2. F; 3. A; 4. C; 5. E; 6. B

PAGE 257

1. bee/tree; 2. Ten/pen; 3. cow/plow; 4. rabbit/habit; 5. gears/shears; 6. witch/ditch

PAGE 258

1. unseen; 2. review; 3. preschool; 4. impossible; 5. misbehave; 6. disagree

PAGE 259

1. review; 2. underwater; 3. misspell; 4. preheat; 5. unhappy; 6. disagree

PAGE 260

1. excitement/retirement/agreement; 2. windy/dirty/noisy; 3. childish; 4. kindness/likeness; 5. friendly/kindly/likely 6. friendship

PAGE 261

1. hugging; 2. jumped; 3. slipped; 4. sliding; 5. hopping; 6. digging; 7. beautiful; 8. smiled; 9. caring; 10. cutting

PAGE 262

1. un forget(table) E; 2. in describ(able) A; 3. misspel(ling) F; 4. un friend(ly) B; 5. un help(ful) C; 6. un control(lable) D

PAGE 263

1. black/smith; 2. danc/ing; 3. zom/bie; 4.vil/lag/er; 5. but/ter/fly; 6. cob/web; 7. em/er/alds; 8. En/der/man

PAGE 264

1. B; 2. A; 3. A; 4. A; 5. B

PAGE 265

1. B; 2. A; 3. A; 4. B; 5. A

PAGE 266

1. apple/bread/butterfly/carrot; 2. clock/emerald/flower/goat; 3. iron/lava/lever/magma; 4. moon/ocelot/orb/potato

PAGE 267

1. B; 2. B; 3. B; 4. A; 5. A; 6. A

PAGE 268

1. ate/eight; 2. meet/meat; 3. knew/new; 4. know/no; 5. their/there/they're; 6. two/too/to

PAGE 269

```
K N I G H T Z Y E R S N R W
N E T H G I E W C L O E D T
J B U Y J D R W A L O A A D
N G R L I Y D H E Y D H D Q
K T B A B R N O P P R T V R
M A T K K Z T L P E H E E S
D J E W Y E X E C G B W R J
R R N R X R L E I W E O Z T
W A I T B L I N O L D Q J T
D E J R T P T U B E Y L T N
O J L V D V L V Z Q M R T L
O K R A K D D B D R B X V D
W Q V J T J L T N G Y K B N
```

PAGE 270

(Steve) farm, animals, cows, sheep, wheat, pigs, carrots, beetroots, chickens, seeds, animals, baby, babies, minutes, (Steve) pens, animals, barn, coop

PAGE 271

1. hissed; 2. attack; 3. explodes; 4. climb; 5. runs; 6. flashes

PAGE 272

Answers may vary. Possible answers include:
1. yellow, spotted; 2. five, white; 3. long, green; 4. old, creepy; 5. cute, pink

PAGE 273

1. Creeper hissed loudly. 2. Iron golem awkwardly handed the flower to the villager. 3. Alex gently cared for the animals. 4. The baby zombie villagers played happily. 5. Alex carefully put the diamond armor in the chest. 6. The bee buzzed quickly from flower to flower.

PAGE 274

1. and; 2. but; 3. or; 4. and; 5. so; 6. but

PAGE 275

1. in; 2. behind; 3. on; 4. under; 5. around; 6. over

PAGE 276

1. Steve collected wood (from) the forest to build a shelter. 2. Steve climbed (up) a tree to get away (from) the mobs. 3. You can find a witch hut (in the Swampland Biome. 4. (Inside) the witch hut, you can find a crafting table. 5. Horses can be found (in) the Plains Biome. 6. If you click (on) a horse, you can ride it.

PAGE 277

1. The Minecraft world has many mobs. 2. You can tame some mobs. 3. Some mobs can be eaten. 4. Creeper likes to screech and explode. 5. Utility mobs can help a player. 6. Iron Golem is a utility mob.

PAGE 278

1. S; 2. F; 3. S; 4. S; 5. F; 6. F

PAGE 279

1. Steve found a diamond, so he put it in his cart. 2. Steve wanted to tame a creeper, but it exploded. 3. Steve can go to the Desert Biome, or he can go to the Jungle Biome. 4. Steve likes to play in the village, but Alex likes to play on the farm.

PAGE 280

1. Zombies are undead hostile mobs. 2. Watch out for baby zombies! 3. Baby zombies are even more dangerous than big zombies. 4. On Halloween, zombies put pumpkins on their heads.

PAGE 281

Cave spiders live ^in abandoned mineshafts. they climb walls and (hid) sp^hide in cobwebs. (The) sp^they all so swim (so) sp^also very fast. They spawn (frum) sp^from monster spawners. They (attak) sp^attack by jumping at (there) sp^their target. They are very poisonous. When killed, they can drop string or spider^a 's eye.

349

PAGE 282

1. bird; 2. bat; 3. dog; 4. horse; 5. mule; 6. bunny; 7. cat; 8. fox

PAGE 283

1. C; 2. E; 3. A; 4. B; 5. D

PAGE 284

1. B; 2. A; 3. B; 4. A; 5. B; 6. B

PAGE 285

1. A; 2. A; 3. B; 4. B; 5. A; 6. B

PAGES 286-291

Answers will vary.

PAGE 292

1. Get a crafting table, five glass blocks, three obsidian blocks, and a nether star. 2. Place the three obsidian blocks along the bottom row of the crafting table. 3. Place the nether star in the center of the table. 4. Place the rest of the glass blocks on the table. 5. Set the beacon on a pyramid to activate it.

PAGE 293

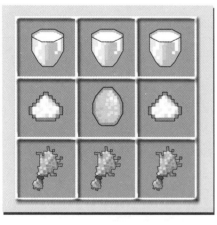

PAGE 294

1. D; 2. C; 3. E; 4. A; 5. B

PAGE 295

1. you need put it in an oven.
2. If you want to trade with a villager,
3. they only will attack if attacked.
4. If you want to tame a horse,
5. you can make rabbit stew.
6. When attacked,

PAGE 296

Answers will vary.

PAGE 297

1. 60; 2. 70; 3. 30; 4. 20; 5. 90; 6. 20; 7. 80; 8. 20; 9. 100; 10. 10; 11. 70; 12. 50; 13. 70; 14. 30; 15. 40; 16. 40; 17. 10; 18. 70

PAGE 298

1. 6,000 + 700 + 20 + 5; 2. 1,000 + 400 + 80 + 9; 3. 8,000 + 40 + 6; 4. 9,000 + 900 + 90 + 9; 5. 4,000 + 300 + 90 + 1; 6. 2,000 + 800 + 10 + 4; 7. 3,000 + 700 + 20 + 9; 8. 5,000 + 600 +2; 9. 7,000 + 900 + 40 + 7

PAGE 299

1. >; 2. <; 3. <; 4. <; 5. <; 6. <; 7. >; 8. <; 9. =; 10. >; 11. >; 12. >

PAGE 300

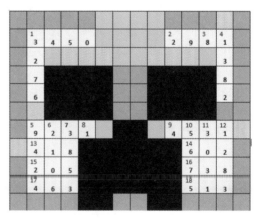

PAGE 301

1. 858; 2. 657; 3. 859; 4. 439; 5. 493; 6. 793; 7. 626; 8. 879; 9. 869

HIS FEET OFF THE FLOOR

PAGE 302

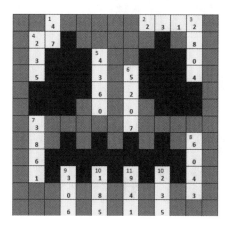

PAGE 303

1. 301; 2. 153; 3. 231; 4. 503; 5. 145; 6. 366; 7. 527; 8. 194; 9. 349

SEE OH DOUBLE YOU

PAGE 304

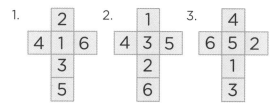

PAGE 305

1. 600 animals; 2. 252 fish; 3. 195 baby polar bears; 4. 1,011 steps

PAGE 306

1. 12/35; 2. 9/8; 3. 13/36; 4. 7/10; 5. 9/18; 6. 15/56; 7. 14/45; 8. 11/28; 9. 7/12

PAGE 307

1. 40/56/48/24; 2. 20/35/45/10; 3. 18/6/8/14; 4. 3/0/7/9; 5. 4/24/32/8; 6. 49/28/35/63; 7. 48/30/6/36; 8. 9/72/0/27 9. 9/15/21/18

PAGE 308

1. 1/20, 10/2, 4/5, cross out 6 and 3; 2. 6/2, 12/1, 3/4, cross out 7 and 8; 3. 24/1, 6/4, 3/8, 2/12, no numbers crossed out; 4. 9/4, 6/6, 2/18, 12/3, 1/36, no numbers crossed out; 5. 7/6, 42/1, 3/14, 2/21, cross out 8 and 9; 6. 1/25; 5/5, cross out 7, 2, and both 9s; 7. 27/1, 9/3, cross out 7, 4, 2, and 6; 8. 5/7, 1/35, cross out 3, 15, 4, and 10; 9. 6/8, 3/16, 48/1, 12/4, 2/24, no numbers crossed out

PAGE 309

1. 1/12, 2/6, 3/4; 2. 1/15, 3/5; 3. 1/18, 2/9, 3/6; 4. 1/24, 2/12, 3/8, 4/6

PAGE 310

1.

3	6	13	4	7	9	43	31	6	8
1	9	15	2	21	5	75	22	10	98
17	53	19	18	35	24	29	40	2	11
46	83	16	26	13	23	27	28	71	62
89	44	95	47	52	65	38	30	70	57
20	78	55	88	14	67	86	33	51	49
59	74	14	42	93	73	77	36	39	68
12	52	22	61	50	25	80	54	37	42

2.

4	8	7	16	14	13	6	19	9	21
30	5	12	2	20	19	27	22	1	42
64	3	10	76	24	35	33	51	17	32
58	14	29	70	28	34	78	53	49	45
90	37	47	32	6	73	86	94	99	50
83	74	43	69	36	11	57	2	25	63
81	39	12	77	51	40	44	48	68	17
61	34	95	76	22	55	66	82	52	56

PAGE 311

1.

5	12	17	21	2	6	19	27	11	8
10	15	24	22	3	9	18	1	7	16
14	13	20	27	30	35	28	33	29	31
72	61	59	25	53	46	40	47	39	37
88	84	66	78	91	94	45	56	58	62
97	92	83	79	69	89	74	50	99	78
28	36	49	52	80	19	83	55	73	81
77	54	48	37	61	93	76	60	65	70

2.

9	18	32	11	31	7	49	8	18	21
1	2	27	3	6	67	19	20	47	36
14	39	40	36	45	10	4	9	5	12
38	29	25	17	54	44	76	13	55	53
50	89	82	15	60	63	98	73	69	70
62	12	28	97	85	79	72	81	37	64
49	21	46	95	23	77	86	66	90	83
84	13	67	30	52	88	80	57	42	99

PAGE 312

1. 45; 2. 450; 3. 450; 4. 4,500; 5. 24; 6. 240;
7. 240; 8. 2,400; 9. 42; 10. 420; 11. 420; 12. 4,200;
13. 4; 14. 40; 15. 40; 16. 400; 17. 18; 18. 180;
19. 180; 20. 1,800; 21. 35; 22. 350; 23. 350;
24. 3,500; 25. 48; 26. 480; 27. 480; 28. 4,800;
29. 12; 30. 120; 31. 120; 32. 1,200

PAGE 313

1. 240/2,400/24,000; 2. 150/1,500/15,000;
3. 270/2,700/27,000; 4. 360/3,600/36,000;
5. 420/4,200/42,000; 6. 610/6,100/61,000;
7. 580/5,800/58,000; 8. 730/7,300/73,000;
9. 860/8,600/86,000; 10. 900/9,000/90,000

PAGE 314

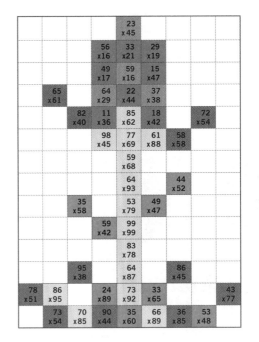

PAGE 315

1. 621; 2. 2,080; 3. 1,978; 4. 750; 5. 4,828; 6. 2,142;
7. 713; 8. 676; 9. 1,749; 10. 1,428; 11. 810; 12. 1,452

HE HAD NO BODY TO GO WITH.

PAGE 316

PAGE 317

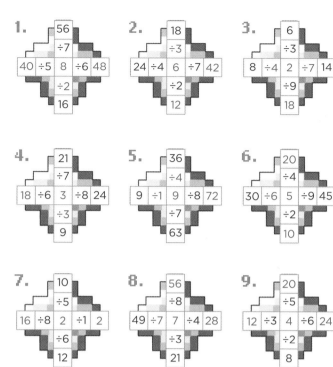

1. 56 ÷7 | 40 ÷5 8 ÷6 48 | ÷2 | 16

2. 18 ÷3 | 24 ÷4 6 ÷7 42 | ÷2 | 12

3. 6 ÷3 | 8 ÷4 2 ÷7 14 | ÷9 | 18

4. 21 ÷7 | 18 ÷6 3 ÷8 24 | ÷3 | 9

5. 36 ÷4 | 9 ÷1 9 ÷8 72 | ÷7 | 63

6. 20 ÷4 | 30 ÷6 5 ÷9 45 | ÷2 | 10

7. 10 ÷5 | 16 ÷8 2 ÷1 2 | ÷6 | 12

8. 56 ÷8 | 49 ÷7 7 ÷4 28 | ÷3 | 21

9. 20 ÷5 | 12 ÷3 4 ÷6 24 | ÷2 | 8

PAGE 318

1. 9 R2; 2. 7 R1; 3. 6 R6; 4. 9 R1; 5. 2 R4; 6. 4 R3; 7. 9 R3; 8. 5 R1; 9. 8 R1; 10. 5 R2; 11. 5 R6; 12. 4 R2; 13. 4 R1; 14. 3 R8; 15. 6 R2

SO IT COULD HAVE A PIGNIC.

PAGE 319

1. C; 2. A; 3. D; 4. B; 5. E

PAGE 320

1. 108 zombies; 2. 5 used 8 of the spawners and 6 used 1 of the spawners; 3. 76 creepers; 4. 90 husks

PAGE 321

1. 126 flowers; 2. 13 books were on 5 shelves and 12 were on 1 shelf; 3. 9 mooshrooms were spawned each day; 4. 2,320 apples

PAGE 322

Exact shading may vary, but number of spaces shaded in should match the examples below.

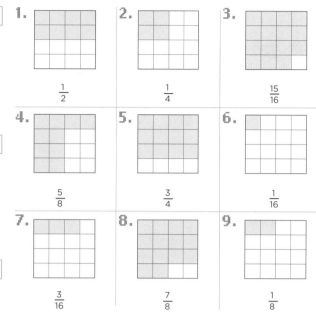

1. $\frac{1}{2}$ 2. $\frac{1}{4}$ 3. $\frac{15}{16}$

4. $\frac{5}{8}$ 5. $\frac{3}{4}$ 6. $\frac{1}{16}$

7. $\frac{3}{16}$ 8. $\frac{7}{8}$ 9. $\frac{1}{8}$

Order: $\frac{1}{16}, \frac{1}{8}, \frac{3}{16}, \frac{1}{4}, \frac{1}{2}, \frac{5}{8}, \frac{3}{4}, \frac{7}{8}, \frac{15}{16}$

PAGE 323

1. D; 2. A; 3. E; 4. B; 5. C

PAGE 324

1. $\frac{7}{9}$ 2. $\frac{8}{8}$ or 1 3. $\frac{5}{9}$ 4. $\frac{8}{9}$ 5. $\frac{3}{4}$ 6. $\frac{5}{6}$

PAGE 325

1. $\frac{3}{9}$ 2. $\frac{1}{8}$ 3. $\frac{2}{6}$ 4. $\frac{5}{9}$ 5. $\frac{3}{6}$ 6. $\frac{2}{8}$

PAGE 326

1. $1\frac{1}{2}$ 2. $\frac{2}{3}$ 3. $1\frac{1}{3}$ 4. $\frac{4}{6}$ 5. $1\frac{1}{4}$ 6. $\frac{2}{3}$

PAGE 327

1. $1\frac{1}{2}$ cups; 2. $\frac{4}{5}$ cup; 3. 1 glistening melon; 4. $\frac{3}{4}$ cup of sugar

PAGE 328

1. .4; 2. .32; 3. .50; 4. .7; 5. .08; 6. .16; 7. .03; 8. .2; 9. .28; 10. .09

.03 / .7

PAGE 329

1. $\frac{6}{10}$, .6;   2. $\frac{28}{100}$, .28;   3. $\frac{3}{10}$, .3;   4. $\frac{6}{100}$, .06;

5. $\frac{56}{100}$, .56;   6. $\frac{81}{100}$, .81;   7. $\frac{1}{100}$, .01;

8. $\frac{1}{10}$, .1;   9. $\frac{58}{100}$, .58

PAGE 330

1. 1; 2. 3; 3. 6; 4. 10; 5. 15; 6. 21; 7. 28; 8. 36

PAGE 331

1. 9/9; 2. 25/34; 3. 49/83; 4. 81/164;

5. 11 x 11 = 121/285

PAGE 332

1. 36′; 2. 26′; 3. 40′; 4. 44′; 5. 32′; 6. 36′; 7. 12′; 8. 36′

PAGE 333

1. 9/4/36; 2. 5/4/20; 3. 6/5/30; 4. 8/1/8 5. 8/4/32; 6. 7/7/49

7. Length times width equals the area. l x w = a

PAGE 334

1. acute; 2. obtuse; 3. right; 4. right; 5. obtuse; 6. acute; 7. right; 8. obtuse; 9. right

PAGE 335

1. right; 2. acute; 3. acute; 4. right; 5. acute; 6. acute; 7. right; 8. right; 9. acute; 10. obtuse; 11. acute; 12. obtuse; 13. right; 14. right

PAGE 336

1. Parallel; 2. line; 3. line segment; 4. ray; 5. Intersecting; 6. point; 7. Perpendicular

PAGE 337

1. Answers will vary.   2.

3. 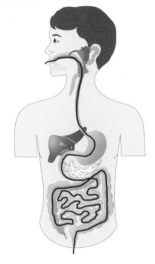   4. Dot to dot will show snow golem

PAGE 338

Answers will vary.

PAGE 339

1. nose; 2. mouth; 3. larynx; 4. trachea; 5. bronchi; 6. lungs; 7. diaphragm

PAGE 340

PAGE 341

Heart is the organ between lungs.
Veins are blue and lead to heart.
Arteries are red and lead away from heart.

PAGE 342

1. Brain
2. Spinal cord
3. Nerves

PAGE 343

```
V E R T E B R A E R D
P R L R X A P S N D T
D A W B I Y C N C N B
R J T B I A C R R Z J
I F I E P D A C T Y P
B T I U L N N S O L B
C Y L B I L U A L C R
A A Y U U I A V M U D
G L M Q D L I D M D Y
E W X A J S A E Z R B
B D R R G D F T P J D
```

PAGE 345

PAGE 346

Answers will vary.

PAGE 347

1. ocelot: predator; cod: prey; 2. shark: predator;
fish: prey; 3. frog: predator; fly: prey; 4. snake:
predator; eggs: prey; 5. wolf: predator; rabbit:
prey; 6. bird: predator; worm: prey